Alison J.D. Adams

On the Dark Side of Ayahuasca

An Illustrated Story of Healing

SilverWood

Published in 2022 by SilverWood Books
SilverWood Books Ltd.
14 Small Street, Bristol, BS1 1DE, United Kingdom
www.silverwoodbooks.co.uk

Copyright © Alison J.D. Adams 2022
Illustrations and photos, except those of the ritual © Alison J.D. Adams 2022
Photos of the ritual © Robyn Fox 2022

The right of Alison J.D. Adams to be identified as the author of this work has been asserted in accordance with the Copyright, Designs and Patents Act 1988 Sections 77 and 78.
All rights reserved. No part of this publication may be reproduced, stored in a retrieval system, or transmitted in any form or by any means, electronic, mechanical, photocopying, recording or otherwise, without prior permission of the copyright holder.

This book is based on a true story, but names, characters, businesses, places, events, locales and incidents have been changed to protect the privacy of any person that might be concerned. Some are the products of the author's imagination or used in a fictitious manner. This book does not recommend taking illegal substances. Any liability for personal injury, property damage or financial losses is excluded. For any medical issues, please consult with your doctor.

Graphic support and cover: picnic grafik-design, www.picnic-design.de

ISBN: 978-1-80042-210-0 (paperback)

British Library Cataloguing in Publication Data
A CIP catalogue record for this book is available from the British Library

ALISON J.D. ADAMS works as a head of department in the sector of flood control and prevention. She loves dogs and nature, especially rivers and lakes. One of her favourite places is the rewilded river Ehen in the Lake District. *On the Dark Side of Ayahuasca* is her first and probably only book. She has always had a love of art, and her paintings and drawings fill large boxes. This is the first time she has shared some of her colourful illustrations with an audience.

Dedication

To Ed Bear and Mr K. who, each in his own way, kept me from going under.

To my partner, Robyn, for accompanying me on the healing journey, for listening to the waterfall of words that needed to be spoken and for helping me to integrate a mountain of stuff.

Thank you!

Disclaimer

I am not an expert on ayahuasca or other hallucinogenic drugs. I have taken ayahuasca only once and I will not take it again. If you have questions concerning hallucinogenic drugs or ayahuasca, I am unable to answer them. My knowledge refers only to this one event.

Warning

Some of the illustrations are expressive and readers may find them disturbing. This is especially the case for 'Anger' on pages 48 and 49, and 'Madness' on page 62. If you are feeling unstable or are easily triggered, I recommend against looking at those particular illustrations.

Table of Contents

Introduction	9
Why did I go on an Ayahuasca Journey?	11
Three Weeks Before – Preparation	15
Thursday – Arrival	17
Friday – The Beginning	19
Saturday – The First Ayahuasca Ceremony	21
Saturday Night Dialogue	29
Sunday – The Second Ceremony	39
Sunday Night Waves	41
Monday – The End/Driving Home	43
Monday – Night Waves	44
Tuesday	46
Tuesday – Night Waves	47
Wednesday	59
Wednesday – Night Waves	61
Thursday	65
Thursday – Night Waves	67
Friday Morning – The End!	70
Robyn	70
Friday Noon – Taking the Fight to a New Level	73
Emergency Admission	73
'Medicinology'	74
Two Weeks in a Psychiatric Clinic	77
Healing the Horror – The Story in Pictures	79
Recipe for a Personal Healing Ritual	82
Last Insight (for now)	88
Thank You Mother Ayahuasca	93
Ayahuasca Horror Trip – Why Me?	94
A Note to the Guides: Don't Push the River	95
Recommendations for Travellers	98
Two Years Later	101
Two Childhood Traumas and their Resolution	102
Literature	104
Acknowledgements	107

Introduction

This book was like some kind of hot potato in my mind that *wanted to come out*. I had a hard time with it because it was always pushing, pushing, pushing me. Now it is finished and I am glad that it is out, and I also kind of like the result.

This book is intended for all those considering undertaking an ayahuasca journey. It is also for those family members and the professionals, such as psychotherapists, who might have to pick up the pieces afterwards. This report 'from the inside' might make the event, and what comes after, easier to understand.

Take care with Mother Ayahuasca. She might more than surprise you. For me, one journey was enough.

And, most importantly, never go on an ayahuasca journey without trusted guides. They protect your body, your sanity and your soul if things go wrong.

Why did I go on an Ayahuasca Journey?

I was in my fifties and had never taken any illegal drugs or psycho-pharmaceuticals in my life. I didn't smoke and hardly ever drank. I was in a stable, long-term relationship and led the responsible hard-working life of a departmental manager with fifty people in my care.

Like many people over fifty, I was looking for healing. I had recently experienced a number of health problems relating to my legs. Some years earlier, due to an injured nerve in my groin that caused great pain with every step I took, I had been almost entirely unable to walk without crutches for a period of over four years. About the time when that was starting to heal, I woke up one morning with a seriously inflamed ankle and was confined to crutches for another year. And, as that finally started to heal, I sprained my ankle on perfectly smooth flat tarmac.

I had the feeling that all of these leg problems had something to do with my constant running. I was a workaholic and always in a hurry, forever ticking items off my long to-do lists. Instead of living, I was merely functioning. I developed problems with my digestion and my hair started to fall out at an alarming rate. For some time, I had been trying to 'heal' my workaholism, but nothing seemed to work. Because of my leg problems I didn't go on holiday for many years and that didn't help my stress levels. I had recently experienced episodes of burnout that really bothered me. It felt as if something was going wrong in my brain. would sometimes wake up in the night to my brain producing an endless stream of senseless word salad. This frightened me and seemed stress-related. I also endured long episodes of sleeplessness, which frazzled my strained nerves even more. Soon, I struggled to remember normal words, such as 'cucumber' or 'telephone', and I started to have difficulty remembering the correct order of letters when writing many common words.

My introduction to ayahuasca as a way of healing came five years ago via a DVD called *For the Next Seven Generations*. The video featured a group of women known as the 13 Indigenous Grandmothers, who hail from the North (e.g., Alaskan Yup'ik), the South (e.g., Gabonese Omyene and Mexican Mazatec), the East (e.g., Nepali and Tibetan) and the West (e.g., Native American Oglala Lakota and Takelma Siletz). These spiritual leaders formed an organisation and travelled the world using their ancient knowledge to bring healing to people everywhere.

Left: Constant Running

The film showed a hospital in the Amazon rainforest where two of the grandmothers worked with ayahuasca as a healing plant.

I was greatly impressed to see terminally ill people healed by ayahuasca tea. The organisation that ran the facility where ayahuasca was administered was the Santo Daime Church. Ayahuasca appeared to be beneficial and many people in this church seemed to take it without any side effects greater than a temporary phase of vomiting. Having watched the DVD, I did some further research and read that ayahuasca can also help with the symptoms of burnout. Ayahuasca is derived from leaves and a plant called *Banisteriopsis caapi*, a giant liana vine from the Amazon rainforest. The video portrayed the tea as a new, almost magical 'herbal tea' with amazing healing properties. It seemed to have only temporary unpleasant side effects, including vomiting. The tea is illegal in some countries but not in others, and the documentaries, books and articles I found were positive in their descriptions of its curative qualities. I tried to find out more about the Santo Daime Church, which has a branch in The Netherlands, but was unable to find a convincing website. The church and its activities lodged in my mind, however, and came back to me some time later when I received some very bad news.

In February 2018, a dear friend was diagnosed with amyotrophic lateral sclerosus (ALS), also known as Lou Gehrig's disease. The medium life expectancy after diagnosis is two years. Western medicine has no cure for ALS. Stephen Hawking was a rare long-term survivor of ALS, but many people do not make it past their second or third year.

My friend's amiable, calm and considerate approach to life had been an enormous inspiration to me for many years and I was utterly devastated when I found out that this wonderful person, who had achieved so much good for so many people in his professional life, had been struck down by such a cruel illness. I wanted to help him and, in March, I wrote to him, asking what he thought about taking therapeutic ayahuasca. He didn't reply, probably because of his strong Christian faith and because taking a non-prescribed drug for its therapeutic benefits was not something he would consider doing. I didn't bring up the subject again because, of course, at that time, I didn't really know what I was talking about. In order to learn about the healing properties of ayahuasca, I thought I should first try it myself. My friend was running out of time, so I couldn't spend another five years simply thinking about it.

Still, I dithered. But in April I met a woman at a fundraising course I attended who had taken ayahuasca and was completely unfazed by the experience. She had vomited a bit, but had experienced no other ill effects. This seemed to be quite an easy way to achieve healing. So, I searched the internet to find out more about the possibility of undergoing an ayahuasca healing experience.

Finally, my partner found the website of an organisation in Duisburg, Germany, which offered guided ayahuasca voyages. This organisation very much appealed to us. They seemed considerate and therapy-oriented, and also practised dance and breathwork (belly breathing, hyperventilation). They even provided tips for the preliminary soup-fasting period. It seemed to be just what I had been looking for. As my own burnout episodes continued, I decided to take the plunge. My partner, however, discovered that someone had died from an allergic reaction to ayahuasca. Given that she has a lot of allergies, she decided not to risk the ayahuasca experience. In the end, I travelled on my own, and in good faith, to Duisburg. What could go wrong with a plant recommended by the 13 Grandmothers?

Three Weeks Before – Preparation

The website for the organisation in Duisburg explained that the substances in ayahuasca interact with many food items that may cause headache and diarrhoea or counter any positive effects of the tea. Therefore, they proposed a special fasting period. Three weeks before the ceremony was due to take place, I started to take the recommended amount of lemon juice mixed with baking soda every morning. The website did not explain why this was necessary, but I took it as general health advice. In addition, for one week before the ceremony, I undertook a soup fast. I was given a long list of food items that I was not allowed to eat during this final week:

- caffeine products (guarana, coffee, tea, cola, energy drinks, etc)
- chocolate
- ginseng, sweet flag, calamus, nutmeg, soy sauce, cultured dairy products (buttermilk, yogurt and cheese)
- dry and fermented sausage (bologna, salami, pepperoni)
- corned beef and liver, meat
- fish, pickled herring and salted dried fish
- eggs, yeast extracts (Marmite, brewer's yeast)
- sauerkraut
- raspberries, figs, bananas, pineapple, avocados, raisins
- nuts
- broad beans and pods (lima, lentils, snow peas and soy beans)
- nose sprays (Vicks, Sinex, Prevalin or Otrivin)

On the evening before I travelled to Germany, I watched the Disney movie *Descendants 2*. The film opened with the sentence, "Let's give Auradon a taste of evil", followed by the mad laughter of Mal, one of the movie's teenage heroines. Had I known what was about to happen, I would have stayed well away from that harmless DVD.

Above: Yenna, Leader of the Ceremony, and Participants Donna, Mette, Alexa, Gülay and Mike

Thursday – Arrival

Duisburg Inner Harbour is the world's largest inland port. It is very busy, but some parts have fallen into disuse and others are reserved for small yachts and private vessels. I had driven about 600 kilometres to a former shoe polish factory that had been converted into a wellness centre, located in a slightly dilapidated but pleasantly relaxed former industrial area. The building stood on the bank of a wide canal that was fed by the river Rhine. For one weekend, this centre was transformed into an 'ayahuasca temple'. I had arrived.

The group consisted of thirty-two people – twenty-five participants and seven guides. We came from all over Europe: Sweden, Norway, Germany, Poland, Switzerland, England, Ireland, The Netherlands, France, Austria, Croatia; and from Syria and Dubai. The seven guides were Yenna, Ed, Vivi, Antonia, Angelica, Gero and Morton. While most of the participants were excited and nervous, two were truly terrified, but still wanted to take the journey. I tried to keep away from the chatter about bad experiences. I didn't want to spoil my experience with all kinds of negative thoughts. Some of the 13 Grandmothers had taken ayahuasca, some of their patients with severe illnesses had been healed by it, and I placed a lot of trust in the Grandmothers and in Mother Ayahuasca. Now I know that I was quite naïve.

Friday – The Beginning

After breakfast on Friday morning, we all sat in a large circle. We were asked to share with the others our feelings and our reasons for being there. Most were too nervous in this circle of strangers to share much. I went along with that energy and didn't say much either.

Next, Yenna, the leader of the ceremony, asked us each to draw an Osho tarot card from the deck. I drew a flower with four petals. I liked this card. In preparation for the ceremony, I had painted a flower at home. It looked very similar to the flower on the card. I took this as a good sign. The text of the Osho card read: "In such a beautiful world we are living in small ponds of our own misery. It is familiar, so even if someone wants to pull you out, you struggle. You don't want to be pulled out of your misery, of your suffering. Otherwise, there is so much joy all around, you have just to be aware of it and to become a participant, not a spectator. Participate in the stars. Participate in the clouds, make participation your lifestyle and the whole existence becomes such a joy, such an ecstasy. You could not have dreamt of a better universe." Yenna drew the Osho card 'trust'. Had I known what was to come, this card could have been a dire warning: Stay out of this ceremony! Something will go wrong and Yenna will very much need to trust her guiding spirits.

Next, we moved on to an activity called heart dancing. Guided by the music and by Yenna, we danced, met each other, smiled at each other and danced with each other in ever-changing pairs. This helped to change the group dynamic, and our energy became warm and friendly. Only Haakon continued to be wracked with fear and his eyes were very large and round. He looked completely terrified.

After lunch and a rest, we came together again for a session of hyperventilation. This intense breathing practice brings you to an altered state of being. I saw it as a test run for the next day's ayahuasca journey. Anyone who could master hyperventilation should also be able to undertake the ceremony. I thought it very considerate of the guides to take us on a test run beforehand. After all, they did not know us prior to our arrival at the centre.

In the evening, I strolled through the main room looking at the paintings and other works of art on the walls. The room was almost like an art gallery. I found two of the paintings disturbing. One was of a dark island full of skulls, with not a single friendly or hopeful image on the large canvas. The other was even more disturbing. The extremely skilled artist had merged several pictures into one, providing multiple different images, depending on your angle of perspective.

From the front, one saw all the chakras and a seemingly harmless woman sitting in a lotus position against a dark background. At the time, I thought this was a painting of Mother Ayahuasca, but today I believe it was actually a painting of the artist. From the side and at a greater distance, the painting turned into a skull surrounded by other skulls. The effect was both alarming and frightening. From the front again, the skulls disappeared without a trace. This had been created by a great artist, and was all the more disturbing for it.

Saturday – The First Ayahuasca Ceremony

At nine o'clock on Saturday morning, we began the ayahuasca ceremony by sitting in a large circle on red mattresses. I was not particularly concerned. Why should I be? I had prepared as I had been instructed, in contrast to some others who had not fasted and seemed to be here more by chance or mistake. I did not even formulate a clear intention of what I wanted from the experience. I decided to let Mother Ayahuasca do what needed to be done.

The ceremony would take about eight hours and would be accompanied by music. Yenna explained that some of us might not feel anything and others might 'journey' straight away. For those not feeling anything, there would be a second and possibly a third cup of ayahuasca later on. She explained that ayahuasca could work on the physical, emotional or cerebral level. Some of us might see things and some might not. Mother Ayahuasca would 'track resistance' in the body and work where she was most needed. By way of introduction, Yenna would lead a half-hour chakra meditation.

We all drank the first cup together. Yenna began to play the music, which sounded like Indian meditation music, flowing and a bit unstructured with some very high-pitched elements. We had just begun to listen to the instructions for the second chakra when my journey began.

First, I saw kaleidoscopic patterns in green and dark pink. Like crystals. It didn't feel particularly nice. Not nice at all. I didn't like it. I didn't want that. Stop! Suddenly, I dropped to my right-hand side, as if I was on a roller coaster. My body started to move on its own. My arms made wide movements and started hitting the floor. Someone put a cushion under my hand. The hitting got harder. Stop! Stop! I lost my conscious mind. I was gone.

Later, Yenna told me about that lost hour. "As I see it, you weren't gone," she said. "You were in a non-ordinary state of consciousness. A state in which the mind mostly plays no role and that's why we rationally can't remember what happened. What you did was move quite viciously with your body while also stating that you didn't want this. Also, you asked, 'Why did I do this?' a couple of times. You were waving your arms a lot and also beating the ground with your hands. Angelica and Gero tried to keep you and the other participants safe as you tried to move through the room. When that didn't work anymore, we decided it would be best for you and the other participants to move you into the adjoining room."

I crawled through the room, but I have no recollection of it. The guides were with me. I realised that they helped me to stand up. They helped me to the next room and onto the sofa. Meanwhile, I was very afraid. And then the *real* trip began. Suddenly, with a roar, and accompanied by a feeling of utter terror, *she* appeared: *The Demon of Pain and Horror and Torture. The Demon Queen of Evil.* She talked in a deformed undulating voice. She had been waiting for thousands of years for this one moment. To incorporate. To return to this universe. She had been waiting for this particular stupid girl, this Little Miss Just-too-perfect, trying to do everything exactly right to get a 'pure' experience. Oh, she would get a pure experience! She was about to inflict so much pain on everybody, oh, to rule the planet, to rule the universe! Stupid ayahuasca people! Stupid girl! They didn't know what they were doing. They didn't know that she had been waiting. Waiting for so long for this one moment. They didn't know in their stupid little temple, that they would release the *essence of evil.*

She snorted at the flower I had painted and the flower tarot card I drew. It was all *fake*. It was all in her plan. To lure me here. To this place. At exactly this time. Fake and true at the same time. There always had to be a first one. And it was me. Oh my god, she had chosen me. I was going to unleash the darkest evil on to the planet! No, no, no! I didn't want that. I did not want that. (I was just a tiny voice in my head.) I wanted to get out of this!

She and I oscillated in waves. Everything was full of kaleidoscopic colours. With every wave, she grew stronger. Oh my god. What had I done?

Left: Start of the Voyage

"Why did I do this? Why did I take this stuff?" Then she took over, and I said, with *her* weird booming voice: "Why did I doOoo that?" Mocking me. Another wave. Shit! Shit! *Shiiitt*! I started hitting the floor again. I started biting myself. Making ugly faces. She was clawing at her surroundings with her claws, strong claws, she was getting stronger and stronger. I told my guides: *"I really need to get out now, please*!"

"Why did I do this? *Why did I do this? Why did I do this?*"

They told me that someone was fetching something. I told them to hurry. There was a dark hole and it was the direct vertical drop into hell, a direct route to an unimaginable box of horrors. I didn't want to fall into this hole. I cried "I don't! I don't! I don't!" but I went under again.

She started talking to them. About pain. SOo much pAin in the world. She wanted to scare them. She was going to destroy this place. *Oh, she was so going to destroy this place!*

I managed to get through and told her and everybody in the room "All the evil in the world. People don't like it. I don't like it. I really don't *like it!* Why are some people evil? I don't understand it. Nobody likes it. Nobody. So why do it?"

By now, I could see that everyone was looking very concerned. Ed was holding my left arm, Gero my right. Angelica and Yenna were there too. They were speaking rapidly to each other in German. I heard the word "ambulance". Although I was only half present in the room and could see the weird waving colours even with my eyes open, I realised that this was not 'normal procedure'. None of the others were doing this. I was the only one. This was not a normal ayahuasca journey. It was something different. I thought: "There is always a first. I am going to be the first one in Duisburg to die on an ayahuasca voyage. My soul will end up in this hellhole, probably for ever." It would have been better to die than plunge into that hole. I was not only fighting for my life and sanity now, but for my soul.

I lost control again and she was back. By now, she had a power of planetary proportions. She was out. She tried to stand up. They held her back. She clawed at them. *"Let me get up! Go away!"* Soon she would stand up with Ed and Gero dangling from her arms like Christmas decorations. She screamed: *"This is the truth!"*

Left: The Demon Queen, the Essence of Power and Evil

She was out of her prison and taking her time now, gathering her strength. Nobody would ever get in her way again. She was big enough now. I could feel the hole getting nearer. Down in this hole, deep deep down, were all kinds of utterly scary faces: zombies; white walkers, like the walking dead from *Game of Thrones;* devils. She was going to push me into this hole, I could feel it. And then I would lose my mind. I was terrified, begging my guides to "*Please get me out immediately!*"

Ed said: "Alison, don't go there. Don't go there. Don't make this ugly face. *Alison, look at me! Look at me!*"

I looked at him.

Or tried to.

But I was so scared that the faces of my guides would turn into grotesque monsters and zombies that I tried to not look at them too much. I would be utterly lost without them. I would lose my mind.

Angelica brought me oranges. I ate them as fast as I could. I was only seconds away from the hole now. I was utterly terrified. I bit into the pieces of fruit like an animal. I asked Ed again: "Please, get me out." He replied: "You are already on the way out now." I didn't feel it. I kept going in and out, and I could feel her enormous power right beside me. I talked and talked. I told Ed everything. Everything that happened. Everything about the doctor and exactly what he did. All the details. I didn't care if anybody heard me. "This is the truth! *This is the truth!*" I even told them about my self-hurting and self-harming with fire, with matches. About the game I invented called *Keep your radiant smile.* I talked and talked and talked. I lost my train of thought again and again, but still I continued talking.

Finally, I could feel that ayahuasca was losing its grip on me. For now. But I could still feel the hellhole. I could still feel *her*. This felt like a pause. She was out of her former prison now and would use the next opportunity to come back. I would never be able to sleep again. And, still tripping, I now knew that there is a hell. All my concepts about death were wrong. Demons exist. They are real. I got out of the horror trip, but I was rattled to the bone.

Ed told me that, from his experience, I went in very deep. Unusually deep. The ayahuasca kept coming in waves, but they were much weaker now. My body shook and moved, but Ed, my bear, and Angelica stayed with me. The ceremony was almost over. Eight hours had passed but, to me, it felt like three.

At the end of the ceremony we were all given a great quantity of melons and oranges to eat. With Ed's help, I limped back into the main room and sat in the main circle. As I looked down at my body, I saw that both of my hands were covered in bruises front and back.

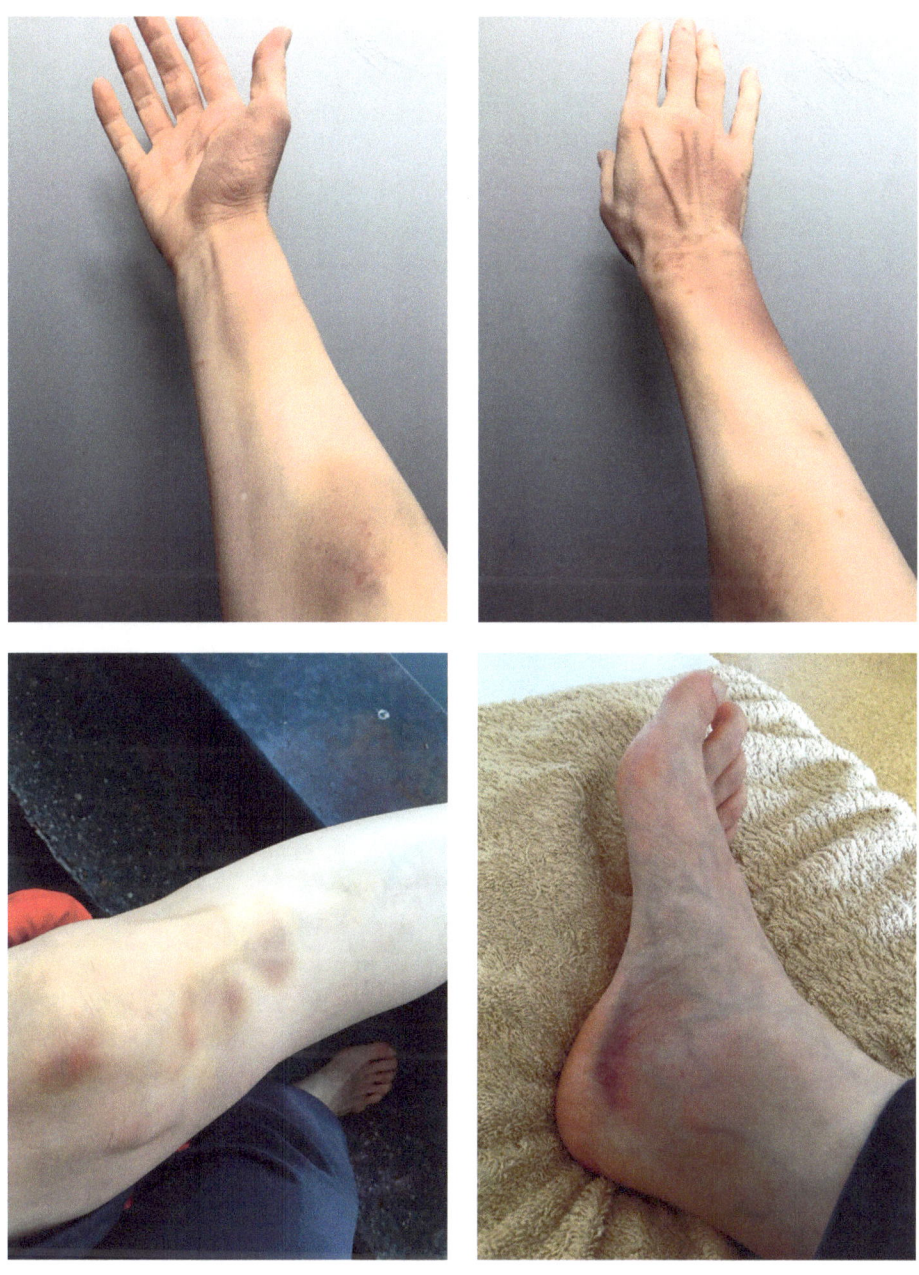

*Above: Directly after the journey everything was black and blue.
My ankles were swollen to elephant size; I couldn't walk anymore.*

I had bruises all over my body: elbows, arms, knees, even my head, nose and chin. I had seriously bitten myself three times. One of my nails was broken. My ankles were so swollen that I couldn't walk. I was glad that I had survived this horror trip and had not fallen into the black hole, but now I could feel the hole at the boundary of my consciousness. We were invited to share our experiences with the rest of the group. It turned out that quite a few people had had unpleasant journeys, but none to the same extent as me. We were asked to say two words. My words were "pain" and "fear".

In the evening, I talked to Yenna. She told me not to fight the stuff. Fighting makes it larger. Makes it stronger. She told me to try and accept it or even love it. I asked her: "How can you not fight the Essence of Evil? How can you love evil?" I didn't understand that. I would not and could not either accept or love an evil demon.

We all ate soup together. As I couldn't walk, I stayed in the big room. A few people came to check on me. Although I was embarrassed about the things I had said, which had been heard through the flimsy curtain separating the big room from the adjoining room where I had been, everyone was extremely and genuinely nice to me. François came by, and then Alexa. We talked for a while. They both told me that they tried to support me "telepathically". I assured them that I would never in my entire life do something like this again. It was such a close call. If it had continued for only a few seconds longer I felt I would have completely lost my mind.

By now, my hands had turned completely black and blue. I was bruised all over. I wondered why people would voluntarily undertake an ayahuasca journey. I had been so naïve. Mother Ayahuasca "tracks your resistances"? And how does resistance look to you? Do you have a resistance against horror? Would you like to meet your worst horror personally in your head? For real? I think not. Who in their right mind would like to star in their own scariest horror film?

The guides came to me one-by-one to thank me. I didn't know what they were thanking me for. Ed, this Harley Davidson biker guy, told me I had done a great job and that I was a strong woman. I didn't feel strong, though. I felt afraid. When I came here, I was mentally okay. Now, I was seriously afraid of the dark.

The guides told me that love and compassion would help. Yenna told me that the things that we push away fight back and grow stronger. If they are pushed away a lot, they can grow to demonic proportions. I didn't understand. How could I not fight horror? How could I not push away terror? How could I love sadism? I still didn't understand.

Yenna tried to convince me to sleep, but I was not going there. Occasionally, I heard dark voices in my head. Derogatory voices, saying ugly things about good people. That friendly people are fake or weak. Antonia came by, smiling, playful, with a basket of fruit balanced on her head. I could feel my face smirking. Derogatory. Not loving. Definitely not loving. The dark one, she was still there, right under the surface of me. I started to talk to Mother Ayahuasca in my head. (Voices in my head – oh oh!) She told me that she still had a bit of work to do. She would tell me when I could go to bed. I wrote down our dialogue.

Saturday Night Dialogue

I knew one thing about the Demon Queen of Pain and Torture: she wasn't there when I was twelve. She appeared when I was thirteen, after I had been to 'the doctor'. I played it out on paper. Drawing torture scenes. But it was never the really heavy stuff, like chain saws. The hero or heroine was always the one being tortured. They were beaten, they were branded and cut, they were tortured with electric shocks. But they were stubborn and proud, and never said anything. I sometimes even faked getting electric shocks as a kind of play. I had no idea why I did that. I had banished this particular memory from my mind. Not the memory as such. That got stored under the label 'dentist', meaning 'unpleasant but necessary experience with a doctor'. But what had been completely erased was the emotional content of the experience with the exception of a profound dislike for that gynaecologist. I knew that my masochistic behaviour was weird and not normal, but I had no idea where it came from. I trusted that one day I would find out why I did that and then it would go away.

What twenty or thirty minutes in a doctor's office can do to your life. Block everything. Make you afraid of people. Turn a self-assured little girl into a recluse. What twenty minutes in a room can do to your body. Turn parts of your body into a hard shell. That's what a physiotherapist once told me: "You lower body is like the shell of a crab." Turn your life into twenty years of severe back pain. Block all the energy. The energy that had now been released in a surge of beating the floor with my bare hands.

I didn't want the damage to be that big. But who was I fooling? The damage was enormous. Ed Bear said I was a strong woman. Perhaps he was just hoping. But at least I was living a halfway decent and beautiful life, despite all this damage.

Why does pain 'down there' affect the personality so much, whereas pain elsewhere, by a seriously incompetent dentist, for example, doesn't affect your character at all? I once saw the YouTube videos of the trial of doctor Larry Nassar [1] (see literature). Many women testified to how he had ruined their lives by touching them and abusing his position as a sports physician. This was the question that came into my head: Why can pain down there turn your whole life into a problem? It mirrors the fact that, for many men, self-esteem seems to be connected to the penis. It seems as if the human self-esteem centre is somehow located down there.

Suddenly I could 'hear' Mother Ayahuasca in my head. "I am healing you," she said.

Fortunately, she had a very rational, plain and normal voice. It felt female. Actually, she felt like a giant snake!

Several days before, at home, and still very much uninformed about the more extreme side-effects of ayahuasca, of all the animals in the world, I wished for a snake to be my 'power animal spirit guide'. But I had been looking for a small, 80 cm water snake, not a 250 kg anaconda. What a joke. I discovered later that people have reported seeing snakes or jaguars during their ayahuasca trips. There was even a large snake painting hanging on a wall in the centre that had been painted by a former participant. The ayahuasca brew contains the essence of a liana vine. Lianas don't talk, so a 'snake' is probably the next best approximation if you are talking to a plant.

I was really not very happy with my healing experience and answered: "Nice façade but deadly contents. I 'survived your treatment' but, to me, it felt like a very close call!"

"I am sorry you had this bad experience but, in order to heal that, to put that straight, there was no other way," said Mother Ayahuasca.

"Okay," I said. "I understand that on a rational level. But how is creating a new trauma going to heal the old one?"

"It wasn't new," Mother Ayahuasca said. "It was still the old one."

The doctor. He was behind all this black stuff. He put a lot of negative energy into me with his small white-hot sizzling flame created by electricity. With his cauterising equipment. Like electro-welding. With the intense stench of burnt flesh. With all that incredible pain. With the complete absence of any anaesthetic. That energy didn't know where to go. I was too controlled. I had too much control over my emotions. I was just thirteen years old, still a child, but trying to be really brave and not flinch from pain.

My mum took me to this gynaecologist because I had just had my first period and she was convinced that from now on, for health reasons, regular gynaecological examinations were necessary. The doctor told my mother that I had a cervical growth that could turn into cancer if not treated and I was to return the following week to have it removed.

If you conduct a Google search for 'cervical growth' you will find articles about cervical cancer, so that part was correct. However, cervical cancer is caused by human papillomavirus, a disease transmitted mainly by sexual intercourse. I asked a friend in the medical profession about it and she confirmed that a thirteen-year-old child who has never had any sexual relations cannot have cervical growth that leads to cervical cancer, as the doctor claimed to be treating.

Today, I know that he was lying. But, back then, neither my mum nor I questioned his expertise. I returned the following week and he cauterised the so-called 'growth' in a long and incredibly painful procedure, with only he and I in the room. I later found out that he had done the same to my mum, and probably to every other woman who ever entered his practice.

In 2019, I conducted a web search for 'cauterisation' combined with 'cervical growth' and found pictures of the – now historical? – medical equipment, including the long steel rod. Only the grey rubber mat was missing. I even found articles about the dangers of smoke. Obviously concern has been raised regarding the toxicity of the surgical smoke electrocautery produces. (see for example [2]). In its 2013 medical procedure guidelines, the World Health Organization (WHO) describes the use of cryotherapy, loop electrosurgical excision procedure (LEEP) and cold knife conization (CKC) in great detail [3]. The WHO loop electrosurgical excision procedure guideline notes that, "in some cases, the patient may have a vasovagal reaction with fainting and plummeting blood pressure", although the WHO gives no reason for that. Why do some patients mysteriously suffer from "dropping blood pressure"? Ever heard of a phenomenon called shock? Stick your palm into the flame of a candle and wait until there is 'surgical smoke' and you might find out why some people faint.

I sometimes wonder whether, in addition to the many good people with high ethical standards, the medical profession attracts not a few psychopaths and sadists. You can cut and burn all day and can even get paid for it. Today, individuals who lack empathy and mirror neurons, i.e. psychopaths, can be identified via a certain FMRI brain scan (functional magnetic resonance imaging (see for example [4]). I believe all new medical students should undergo such a scan to prevent them from studying medicine and thus reaching positions of power over especially vulnerable other human beings. Even if some can control their impulses [5] many others do not.

To all the women out there who may one day be treated for so-called "cervical growth" or for real pre-stage cervical cancer, my recommendation is: If it hurts – scream! Scream the roof down! You may be impolite, you may be inconvenient, they may humiliate you, but they will no longer be able to treat you without the use of painkillers. Go to a hospital and get a proper anaesthetic. It will take longer and it will be more expensive. This is why they won't want to do that. Just insist. Don't let a cost effective small procedure that can be performed in any local office setting [6], [7] ruin your love life, your health and your psyche.

Back in the main room on Saturday night, struggling with the effects of the tea and talking to Mother Ayahuasca in my head, another thought popped into my mind. I thought maybe this was a close miss in another way. I suddenly thought that perhaps something serious had befallen my brain and Mother Ayahuasca had taken it out. Allowed it to express itself. Something dangerous. Something evil. I didn't even want to write that down. I was really very scared of this dark shit coming back.

"It is because your good qualities were all *fused* – totally – with this black stuff," said Mother Ayahuasca. "I couldn't free them without working on the dark stuff as well."

"Thank you," I said. "But I still have the feeling that the black energies, the black shapes, might come back. The Demon Queen has so much power. The ultimate power to destroy. Kill. Hurt. I am scared."

"Expressing is releasing!" said Mother Ayahuasca.

"Why am I still feeling *her* in there then? *She* seems to be still inside."

"Yeah. You didn't go to the centre of the blackness, so there might be something left," said Mother Ayahuasca. "Just express it and it will go away. Paint! Paint it and burn it!"

"Actually," I said, "my body doesn't feel better now. It feels worse. Everything is hurting."

"Tell your body it did a great job accompanying you into the dark energy," said Mother Ayahuasca. "Staying alive. I am going to let you know when you can go to sleep."

"Okay," I said. "As long as it doesn't take weeks."

"Don't be afraid," said Mother Ayahuasca. "I will tell you when you can go to sleep."

"Thank you," I said. "You are the voice of reason in all this crazy stuff. Nobody normal wants to be evil. I don't want to be evil."

"This is not about you becoming evil," said Mother Ayahuasca. "It is about you becoming self-empowered. Okay? He was evil. He really was. You tried to get rid of him many times but he still stayed in there. I hope I can get rid of him and his stuff once and for all. Your Rapist. He was a disgrace to his profession as a healer."

"Thank you," I said. "That would be great. But I can still feel the dark energies move around inside."

"Yes. This is part of the process," said Mother Ayahuasca. "Your process. You went four times as deep as everybody else. So, it will take just so much longer to recover."

"What a stupid – maybe brilliant – idea to come here," I said. "Why is there so much fear now, when back then at the doctor there was only pain? There was no fear back then, because I was totally unsuspecting. Maybe I was a bit concerned when he fixed me to his chair with those leather straps, but I didn't expect to be burnt alive. How do you integrate fear?"

"You can only release it," said Mother Ayahuasca. "Your experience created a frame. Evil pictures got stuck to this main frame because they stick to the negative energy that is in there. This is why they tend to collect. Tend to form a collection. If you see something on TV that makes you afraid, such as zombies or other horror figures, this is mainly fear. Fear of something utterly ugly and evil. I guess you have been collecting the fear during the past four decades. It is an addition. A later addition. If the main frame is gone, all the fears can fall away."

"I am thinking about power," I said. "Power generates respect. I respect Ed because he looks really powerful. Weak people don't gain respect. I feel mainly weak."

"You wanted to change," said Mother Ayahuasca.

"But I didn't want to change into the Queen of Evil and Torture and Zombiedom," I said. "Can it dissolve even if I didn't do the last stage, the hellhole?"

"Yes," said Mother Ayahuasca.

"I am very relieved to hear that," I said. "But I am still very, *very* scared. It is one thing to talk to you on some kind of rational basis, but it is another to actually see these dark energies and then feel them lurking in the background all the time. I am also a tiny bit embarrassed in front of the group. Everybody knows all the evil stuff now. It is out there. Everybody heard it. But the truth is the truth. So, that's it."

"These are *your* truths," said Mother Ayahuasca. "There are a million truths. But to you, there is just one: Your truth. And if you don't stay with your truth, part of you dies. And truths may change. Because they are alive. The black hole was full of horrible faces and skulls. Death is usually depicted as a skull. But skulls are 'the truth' of decay, not of death. Beings that die don't turn into skulls the second they die. They still have their own beautiful face at death. So, a skull is not a symbol of death at all. This is not true. This is the thing about personal truths: You can have one – a fearful skull – and then suddenly you can have another – a beautiful woman's face."

"I can't see the skull anymore," I said. "So at least this truth about a fearful thing has just changed. Which could be a very small new truth. Fear released. Fear gone. A totally different picture! A beautiful picture instead of a frightening one."

"If someone speaks his or her truth, it might sound like *the* truth because it is *the* truth for them," said Mother Ayahuasca. "And therefore, you may believe that person. But it was only his or her truth. So be careful of people influencing you with their truths. You always have to check your own truth."

After this conversation with Mother Ayahuasca, people began to return to the main room for the night. I thought I would need earplugs because of the snoring that would occur with twenty-five people sleeping in one room. But how could get hold of earplugs? I couldn't walk. My ankles were swollen to elephant size. It even felt as if I had hurt my nose! François turned up seconds later and asked if I wanted some earplugs from his colourful collection. What a friendly coincidence.

During the night, I couldn't sleep. I was terrified of dreaming, so I stayed awake. Gero volunteered to sleep next to me. It felt good to have a guide beside me. I continued to write stuff down.

I said to the dark thing lurking at the corners of my mind: "You are going to be released. You are going back to where you came from. Back to this guy, this doctor. He needs to deal with you. You are his problem. He made you my problem, but I am not going to carry his crazy stuff for him any longer! *Do you hear me?* Just get out! Get out of this body. Evaporate or go to your *maker!*"

"No. I am the Black Queen of the Universe," said the dark thing.

"You think you are," I said. "But, actually, you are painful energy, a painful memory created by a sadist. This is the Truth. You value the truth. And you know it is true. How can the Queen of the Universe be created by one tiny human sadist?"

"She can still be the ultimate Queen of the universe," said the dark thing. "Incredibly powerful."

Mother Ayahuasca joined the conversation. She said, "In someone who is very controlled, like you are, my dear, it can reach the demonic stage. Still, I'm also glad that you didn't go there."

I asked her: "Why is there so much pain in the world?"

"It is you humans, doing so much wrong," said Mother Ayahuasca. "I don't

particularly like to go there myself, to pain and rape and violence and torture. But how can I heal you otherwise? The concept of Good and Evil, Yin and Yang – half white, half black – it is untrue. If half the world was evil it would be a totally horrible place. It is not half evil. It is more like two to five per cent".

"Unfortunately, with seven billion people on the planet, two to five per cent is still a lot. Good and Evil is a human concept," said Mother Ayahuasca. "Humans invented the dualism, black and white. fifty-fifty. Yin and Yang. But I am NOT from China or Tibet. I am *Amazon*."

One or two hours passed and it was dark. The bad stuff came in waves. I didn't know what time it was, but every time I thought I had gained some control, the fear and panic bounced back and the dark voices rose at the border of my consciousness. I was so glad that Gero was sleeping beside me. These guides were incredibly courageous. They knew things like this could happen and still they did it. The Other was creeping up again.

"It is satisfying to torture you with horror images," it said. "This is fun."

"Get out!" I said. But I was not strong enough to get rid of it.

"I know it is the Truth," said the Other. "I was created by this guy. But I can still be powerful."

Fear was building up again. Fear of finally falling into the hellhole of ugly faces. Fear of losing my mind after all. If you see and feel something so vividly, you can't forget it. You cannot forget those images.

Mother Ayahuasca joined the conversation again. "I am a healer," she said. "I take you to the limit. I take you to the limit of terror, pain, fear and loneliness. But I don't kill people." I didn't care what she said anymore. I was unable to trust her anymore. I was close to panicking. The Other was creeping up. I shouted at it in my head, trying to heed Ed's advice: "I say no to you. I hear you but I'm not taking you in anymore. I am a shining soul!"

I talked to the sadist doctor and his horrible energies: "All this shit was your shit. I send it all back to you! Return to sender! I say no! You cannot come in. I have loads of energy. I could 'rule the world'! And I will keep you out from now on. I hear you. But you can't come in anymore. *This is the truth.* You have to go somewhere else. Actually, I don't really care what you do. *Let go!*"

"Everyone will die eventually," said the Other, "and then I will get you."

"I was never much afraid of death," I replied.

"Oh, you haven't seen Death," said the Other. "He is horrible."

"This is *not* true," I said. "I have seen him. He was blue. So, don't tell me I don't know Death. He is friendly and he saved my life."

Left: Shining Soul

But my conviction was fading. I had always felt I knew that the idea of purgatory was not true. I had been so sure. But now I was so afraid of it being true after all.

"If you are really the Queen of all Evil, why did you only hurt me?" I asked, "This is not particularly evil. You did not hurt the guides. No one got bruised except for me." There was no answer from the Other.

Mother Ayahuasca spoke again. "Shatter this idea of 'a horrible death' on the floor. Let it shatter into one million pieces. The River Rhine will carry it all away, under the bridge, down the river. It will erode the pieces, it will dissolve them, until nothing is left and the fear is gone."

I repeated this like a mantra and it helped me through the wave of darkness. This mantra was going to help me through endless 'discussions with dark forces' in the time to come.

Below: Fire and Pain and Water

At the age of thirteen, when I was in the doctor's treatment room and couldn't cope with the pain anymore, I cried out. But the doctor told me I was a sissy. He humiliated me. He said, "Only twenty more." Now I realise that this number twenty means it was fake. He made it all up. Twenty is too large a number to define exactly. It could have been nineteen or twenty-one if he was actually treating something real down there. You can say 'three'. But you cannot say 'twenty'. After exactly twenty more burnings, he stopped.

Mother Ayahuasca told me: "You need to stay out of the heat. Cool your feet. Stick them out of bed. This is why you go to Oslo or Scotland on holiday and never to Spain or Italy. This is why you don't like tea or hot drinks, especially in the morning. Because of all the fire in you. You need to stay cool. Stay true to yourself."

Sunday – The Second Ceremony

On Sunday morning, we were once again all in the main room, sitting in a large circle on our red mattresses. I had decided to take part in the ceremony, but rather than drink the ayahuasca brew, I would merely observe the others in an attempt to gain a deeper understanding of it all. Each of the others took the journey for a second time. None of their negative experiences were bad enough to prevent them from doing it again. I, on the other hand, would never take ayahuasca again. Not in ten lifetimes.

The second ceremony was identical to the first. The music played and everyone received their cup. I sat there, watching the proceedings. Françoise started to dance by himself. Mike, my neighbour to the right, started to chuckle and giggle. Most of the others lay silently on their mattresses, in a trance or waiting for the tea to kick in. Haakon had looked relieved after his first journey and joined the second ceremony in a much better mood. He was silent as well. It could have been boring to watch the participants lying there for eight hours, but I was very much occupied with myself. I hadn't slept the previous night and I was still moving in and out of waves of fear. I did not write these down. During one such wave, I experienced a very acute fear of losing my mind, of becoming psychotic. Ed came and lay down with me and held me. I was so afraid. Later, I was able to push that idea away and I felt strong and secure once again. After the ceremony, we had a brief opportunity to share our thoughts among the group. My two words on this occasion were "truth" and "trust".

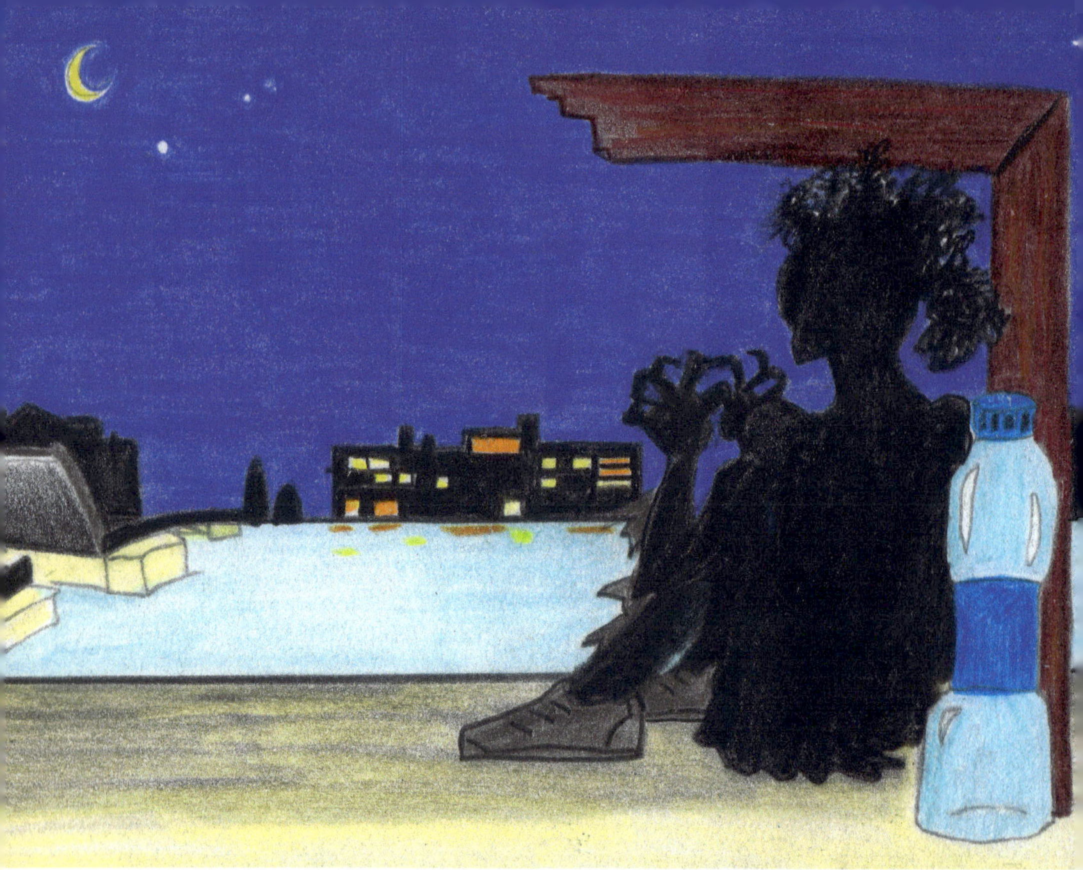

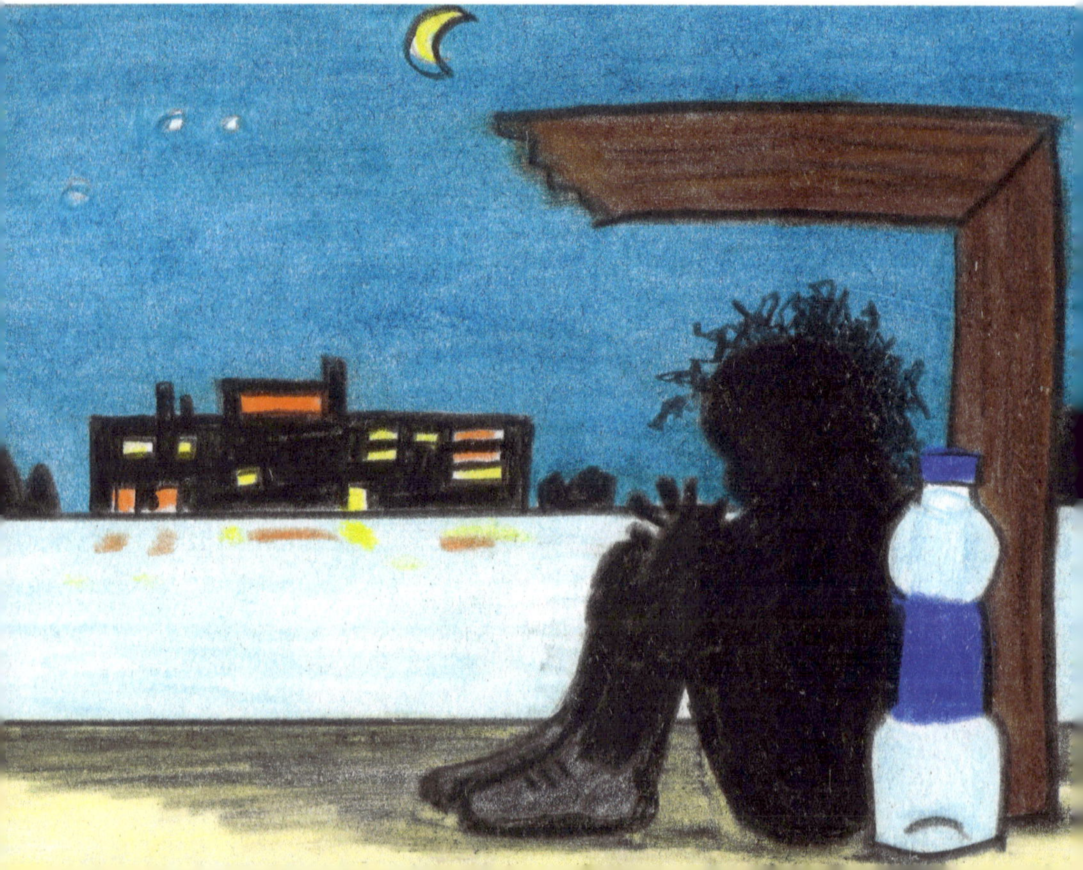

Sunday Night Waves

The night proceeded like the day. I did not sleep and moved from wave to wave. It was about midnight when another panic attack descended on me. This was not about death or horror or evil, but about fire. I saw Vivi in the kitchen and went to talk to her. Leo came along too because Mike was snoring so loudly. I told Leo and Vivi about the doctor and everything he had done to me. About the burning and the fire. Vivi gave me the idea of using water to heal fire. I filled an empty plastic bottle with water and carried it with me like a safety token to mark my boundary, because fire can't cross water. It worked! I felt safer and better.

Leo suggested "Letting go", which I thought was a better idea than Ed's suggestion that I say: "No, go away, you are not mine!" 'Letting go' is soft, slow, tender. It has a completely different energy to 'no!', which is a fighting word. Fighting strengthens these energies. It acts like a mirror. The more you fight, the stronger they become. From behind the bottle, I talked to the fire energy about letting go. I started to feel much better and returned to the main room. But Mike was snoring beside me as if he wanted to flatten a forest. Sleep was impossible. I took my sleeping bag and lay down on the sofa in the kitchen. But sleep continued to evade me.

A dark, fearful thing came in the early hours of the morning. It looked like a burnt corpse. Thankfully, I was shielded by my bottle of water. I told the dark energy to let go of the pain and the anger. We talked for a very long time.

Suddenly, the burnt thing turned into a little 13-year-old girl. *My little girl.* All black and burnt. We had been split into two pieces that day in the doctor's office. She stayed with the pain, frozen in time. I lived on. I told her that I did not choose the side I had landed on. The living, breathing side. We got split in two and I was the lucky one. I tried very hard to reach her, to save her with years of therapy. I even believed I had saved her! I didn't know that the part I saved was not the only part that had been frozen. There were more.

This is what we wrote down together; this is the solution that brought it all together:

If babies or children are tortured, a part of them, a part of their life-force, freezes. It gets frozen in that moment of excruciating pain. The person is split into two pieces. A frozen one and one that lives on.

Left above: Burnt Corpse
Left below: Thirteen-year-old Girl

The frozen one is stuck in a hellhole. It can be stuck there for a very long time.

If you are tortured with fire for more than forty years, you can get deformed and extremely angry. Everybody else is living their lives in harmony, and you are stuck in pain and nobody sees you.

You can get so angry about that. You can hate people for that. You can want to give them a taste of what you are experiencing all the time. If you hurt them, this will only be a fraction of what you are going through. Or, like with us two, if you hurt the part that is still living.

The little girl didn't die in that hellhole. Instead, she became strong and powerful! She became so powerful that she grew to the proportions of a demon queen. She could have killed me. But she didn't want to. Because that would have killed her too.

Growing to demonic proportions has nothing to do with resistance. Instead, it has to do with pain and anger and being stuck in a hellhole for many years. You either die or you become a twisted deformed demon who is still the little child, but in a form twisted by constant pain. Blackened and burnt and still alive. She can become so large and powerful and deformed that you do not recognise her when you meet her. You might think she is an alien. But she is not. She has simply become disproportionate and grown out of shape in her hellhole.

If you ever encounter a demon within you, it is quite probably a part that has been frozen in extreme pain for a long time. Now that my demon, my little girl, has been released, we can both start to let go of the pain, the hatred, the deformation and the anger. We can start to heal.

Thank you, Mother Ayahuasca.

This was the end of our letter. I felt so much better. It had all come together. I now understood what had happened. I was very relieved.

Monday – The End/Driving Home

I drove home in a good mood. My swollen feet could move the pedals although I could barely walk. Everything had fallen into place at last. I felt a tiny bit wobbly on the motorway, but concentrating on something other than what had happened in the preceding days did me good. The only concern was how I would explain my new 'look'? How could I explain all these bruises to my employer? I would have to think of some sort of explanation. But everything would be okay. I would get a good night's sleep and go back to work tomorrow as planned. I couldn't have been more wrong.

Monday – Night Waves

Monday night. Robyn was still visiting her sister in Greece and would come home on Wednesday night. The waves of fear returned. I spent the first half of the night wide awake, then slept for an hour. I dreamt of a mechanical guy, moving at a speed twenty times faster than a normal human being, but in a mechanical way. He had an axe and chopped off my head. I woke up. I told him that he didn't have to do that. That he could let go of the pain, the anger, whatever it was. That he could walk into the river and let go of all of this and that he could be a beautiful man. Like Ed, like François, like Haakon. He walked into the river. I followed him and put my hand on his back. He cried out. He was desperate because the human race is killing nature, is killing the planet. I cried too. He wanted to kill them all. And he wanted to start with me. He let go of his axe and the river washed away the blood. He moved away, still walking in the middle of the river, downstream.

During the next wave, a guy with a chainsaw cut into me. His head appeared to be empty. He reminded me of the big evil fellow in the movie *Fargo*, who put a body into a wood shredder to destroy the evidence. I tried to talk to him, but it was difficult, and he faded quickly after that.

Below: Mechanical Man
Right: Desperation – The River is a Healer

Above: Screw Top

Tuesday

In the morning, I slept again for a few minutes. I dreamt that I was a shaman and screwed off my own head. I had no idea why I did that. I awoke with a start.

Later in the morning, I went to see a doctor because of my swollen ankles and my bruises. I could hardly walk and had to use my old crutches. I invented a story of getting into a fight at a disco in Duisburg at the weekend. The doctor signed me off sick for the rest of the week. I was relieved that I didn't have to show up to work like this, all black and blue. And now my feet were turning purple.

I wrote an email to Yenna: "I had a bit of a rough night on Monday," I wrote. "There were five waves, quite intense, with a lot of bad stuff and I almost called you at the 4 o'clock wave. But knowing that you were there made it possible to get through on my own. It still keeps coming and going. Do you think you could handle being my emergency contact again tonight?" She agreed. She also told me that gardening or doing something outdoors could be beneficial.

Tuesday – Night Waves

First wave: Hatred, Anger, Roaring Anger

I didn't write this down. It was too frightening at the time, but I later painted two pictures: deadly anger, the monster shape; and livid anger, the authentic, healed shape.

After the wave of anger subsided, I suddenly saw myself in my mind's eye with my little burnt black girl cradled in my arms. I started to cry. I was so sad to see her like that. I felt so much love for this tough burnt little girl. It was a healing moment.

Next Two Pages: Deadly Anger and Livid Anger

Second wave at 1.15am.: Deformation

Suddenly, my little girl tried to claw my face away. Rip it away. Shred it. She felt so deformed. So ugly. I tried to tell her that she could let go of her anger, her hatred, if she wanted to. Let it be healed.

During my first appointment with the doctor, I had to undress. When he looked at me, he told me I was deformed. He seemed to be utterly appalled, almost recoiled, when he first saw my tiny new breasts: "Oh my God! You have a funnel chest!" (He meant *pectus excavatum* although I haven't got a clue what he saw back then. Today, my breasts look totally normal and actually quite pretty.) At the age of thirteen, I didn't like my new breasts because I thought they meant I could no longer become a cowboy or an astronaut and had to become like stupid Marilyn Monroe, always acting dumb and in need of rescue. As a kid, I despised her. The doctor's immediate and strong emotional reaction made me feel totally deformed.

There was already so much wrong with me, according to my mum. I had jug ears. She wanted me to have an operation because of that, but I told her they were my heritage from my grandfather and I wanted to keep them. Still, I knew they were too large. I had 'shark teeth', meaning that one tooth on the bottom row at the front was set forward due to a lack of space. No-one could see it, because the bottom row is smaller than the top row, but she wanted me to have an operation on that too. But I defended my teeth. They were *my* teeth after all. I also had knock knees, flat feet and thin straight hair and did not carry myself in the right way. This 'hole in my chest' was the last straw. I was obviously really very ugly. Deformed.

In the subconscious, there is no concept of time. Everything is there at the same time. There is no sense of, "But that was forty years ago!" Time doesn't matter. So, now I had to talk to the little thirteen-year-old girl about deformation. I told her to let go of the idea of being not beautiful, of being ugly, horrible, of wanting to destroy my face.

I told her: "Deformation is not true anymore. There has never been a funnel chest. There has never been a hole in your chest. That was never true. Actually, these breasts are quite nice and beautiful, even after over fifty years. The authentic is beautiful. Always. You are actually beautiful. You can be beautiful if you let go of the negative ideas. Shatter these ideas of deformation on the floor. Let them shatter into a million pieces. The River Rhine will carry them away, under the bridge, down the river. It will erode the pieces, it will dissolve them, until nothing is left and the deformation is gone."

Left: Healing

Burnt Body and Face, Jug Ears, Shark Tooth and Knock Knees

Authentic Beautiful Form

Third wave: The Truth is One

For a change, this was a philosophical wave, with insights from Mother Ayahuasca. She said to me: "There is no duality. There is no dark queen who controls the bad things and no white goddess who controls the good things. There is just a universe full of matter that is *not* under any control. There are not two spirits, like good and bad or white and black. There is only *one*. All is just one enormous field of love, beauty, harmony. On a spiritual level, there is only *one*. There is only one Great Spirit. The Truth is *one*.

"On the level of matter, there is no control. No good control, no bad control. Things move, collide, miss, join, meet, separate, move. In a moving universe, matter moves around without intention. Colliding, spreading, separating, fusing. Much of the evil in the world, much of the pain, like an asteroid hitting a planet full of life forms, is simply matter happening. If you have matter that moves and no control, it happens. You can have a static universe or a moving universe. In a static universe, control is unnecessary. In a moving universe, control is impossible.

"With life, there is intention and the wish to control one's environment. In a universe where matter is moving, all living beings enact control. For example, plants wish to control their surroundings with root poisons, with fast growth for sunlight, with beautiful or inconspicuous appearance, with camouflage. Beings try to control. A single-celled paramecium tries to control its pH by moving away from acidic surroundings. Mammals control their body temperature. Without control, no life. Natural control is necessary and good. Every living being needs and wants control. This is normal within certain boundaries. But they can only live in a moving universe and therefore control is ultimately impossible. Or only possible on a small scale and for a limited time. Until something big or small moves into the way on a collision course. People put 'spiritual intention' behind that and then question the truth of the *one love*. And take it as an excuse to cause collisions themselves, picking up on this perceived 'ill intention' of the spirits, of the universe.

"Humans are the only living forms on this planet that can be evil because they are the only ones who can take control to a conceptual level. Because of their brain. Evil exists only among humans because they are the only ones evolved far enough out of instinct and emotion to pick up on the concept of control in a philosophical way. To consciously try to spread it or test it or get satisfaction out of it. Evil humans take control to new levels."

Left above: The Truth is ONE
Left below: Matter Moving and Dualism

Above: Death / Below: Water is life

"They want, they need, they like and they lust for control. This is the essence of evil – the lust for control. A control that has grown out of all its natural proportions. From a healing perspective, most evil humans can let go of evil. They can revert to the authentic form, the shining soul. Some are mad because of 'matter moving'. A brain can be damaged in a bad way, can lose all compassion, all love. The trapped soul needs to return to the source.

"All the horror, all the evil, all the ugliness lacks essence. It is only conceptual. It is something you have to let go of or can let go of. If you want to come back to love. To the Beauty Way. The Navajo are right. After death, the bad 'chindi' ghost deteriorates into nothingness, because it is just a concept, without essence. The soul dissolves into the ONE. Dualistic concepts are wrong. There is no dualism in the world. Just millions of possibilities.

"Creatures that rely on vision tend towards dualistic concepts. They open and close their eyes; they see or do not see; there is light or darkness; there is good or bad. Their brain creates a binary world. Dogs and snakes would never think like that. Their world is a continuum of smell. A dualistic world view is something artificial. It is wrong."

Fourth wave at 4.20am: I Want to Kill You!

Again, I became extremely terrified. This time the dark energy wanted to kill me. After much debate with myself, I pushed my pride aside and called Yenna in Duisburg in the middle of the night. My body wanted to stop breathing. I had done that when I tried to kill myself at the age of twenty-one. Back then, I was depressed to the brink of suicide. One night I tried to kill myself by simply stopping breathing. And it worked! With every spasm of 'not-breathing' I went down, down, down into myself, using my pain as a sinking anchor, until I reached the beginning of the tunnel with the light on the other side. Then I 'heard' a friendly voice telling me that, if I went any further, the way back to the surface would be too far. That I could not return. I decided to turn around and come back up to the surface. I lay there for a long, long time, still not breathing, and it was extremely peaceful and beautiful. It took a real conscious effort to start breathing again. But finally, I did it.

So, the topic this time was another trauma, but it was probably very much connected to the 'doctor', because why was I so depressed at the age of twenty-one? I told the death figure to let go of not breathing. Just let go of it. Let the River Rhine take it away. It worked after a while and the urge to stop breathing subsided.

Wednesday

On Wednesday morning, an amazing thing happened. My hair stopped falling out. There wasn't a single hair in the bath tub that morning after I washed my hair.

When I phoned my colleagues at work, I was aware that I was more determined. Friendly, but determined, instead of timid, like I used to be. This was new.

I worked during the day doing financial calculations in my home office. I experienced several small waves during the morning but, this time, only in the belly.

> The little girl was healing.
> Her hair had grown back.
> Her hands had healed.
> Her body had healed.
> Only her face was still a burnt and blackened monster face.
> But the healing process was progressing.
> I danced with her.

At about three in the afternoon, the ayahuasca picked up the pace again. A severe wave. Fear peaked again. I researched DMT poisoning (N, N-dimethyltryptamine, the hallucinogenic amine of ayahuasca) on the Internet [8] and texted Yenna to ask if there was medical help available. She said there was no 'antidote'.

I took her advice from the previous day and went outside to do some gardening. It was warm and softly raining. I was wet and warm and glad to be outside. I weeded around the wheelie-bin area and on the curb of our street. It took me an hour to get away from the fear and I stayed outside until 7pm.

Immediately after the first ceremony on Saturday, I had had the unsettling feeling that there was something alive in my body, that something snakelike was slithering around among my internal organs. For the next few days, I had glimpses of this weird and unsettling feeling. While weeding the curb, I suddenly had an insight: "I actually have a large snake inside me. Seven meters long. My intestines! When they move, they cause this snakelike feeling. I have been afraid of my own intestines! Their movements, their hot juices, their house cleaning."

Intestines are responsible for *shit*. They process shit. In the widest sense, they process all things shitty. They probably also process mental shit. Much of the tension that had built up over the day now flowed away from me. The intestines have quite a large brain and one of the biggest nerves, the vagus, connects the intestines and the stomach with the brain in the head. Mother Ayahuasca had obviously targeted my intestinal brain too. To process the accumulated shit. That was why the fasting was so important. Because intestines that are busy have no time for major housecleaning. This was why, in bad situations with ayahuasca, fruit helps. Fruit sends a positive signal to the intestine-brain. There are things that the intestine-brain really likes, such as good tastes. It was my own belly that made me feel as if I had something alive in there.

Later, when Robyn arrived home from the airport, she was shocked to hear and see what had happened. I tried to keep it together. But, a long time ago, Robyn had a friend who became psychotic and she knew the signs: I had to sleep alone with the lights on, with my water bottle and other positive symbols surrounding me in a circle. I was acting weird. Robyn was very concerned, but kept her concerns to herself. There was not much she could do.

Wednesday – Night Waves

I wrote down very little of what happened on Wednesday night. But the topics were trust, madness and sorrow. Here are some pieces of conversation that I remember from that night:

"Trust cannot be forced," I said. "Trust grows. You do not make it by pulling at it."

"Trust will be there, eventually," said Mother Ayahuasca. "Trust in the *one*. Trust in the eternal enormous love."

"I can't go to work," I replied, "because I am all wobbly. You said that I would be okay by now. You said I would be okay in a short while."

"I am a plant," said Mother Ayahuasca. "You are an animal. You are so fast. What do you mean by 'in a short while'? To me your slow is just a shade of fastness. As a plant, I can't be that precise. Which exact shade of fastness do you want? I cannot be that precise in my predictions about someone who is a thousand times faster than me."

Left: Trust / Next two pages: Madness and Sadness

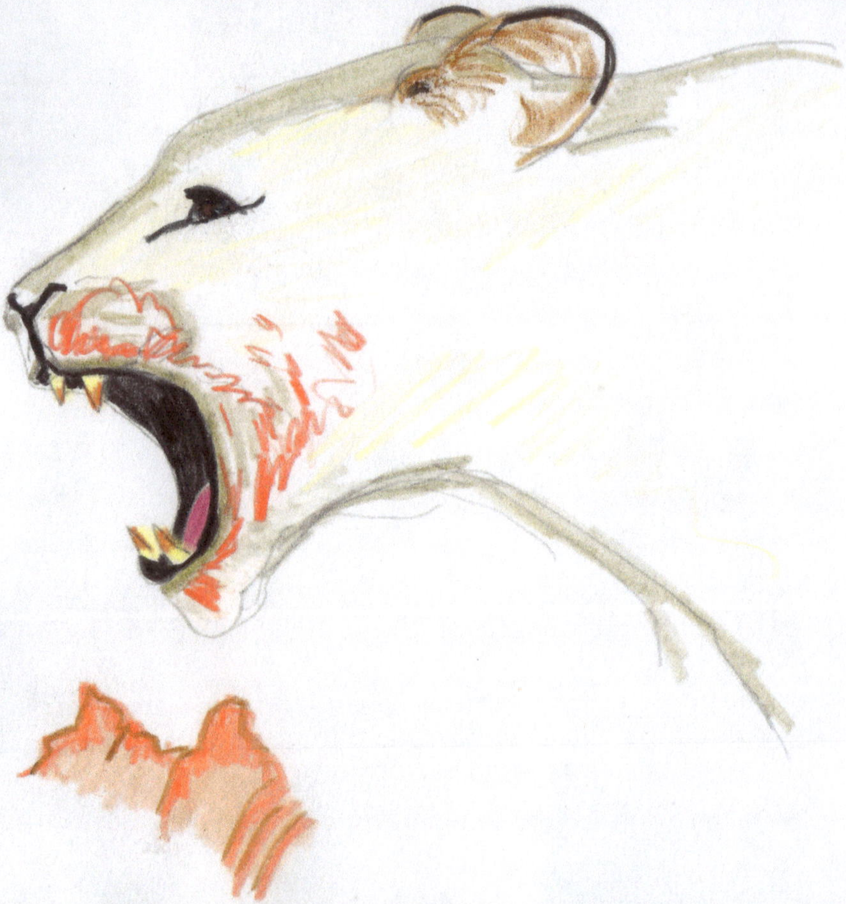

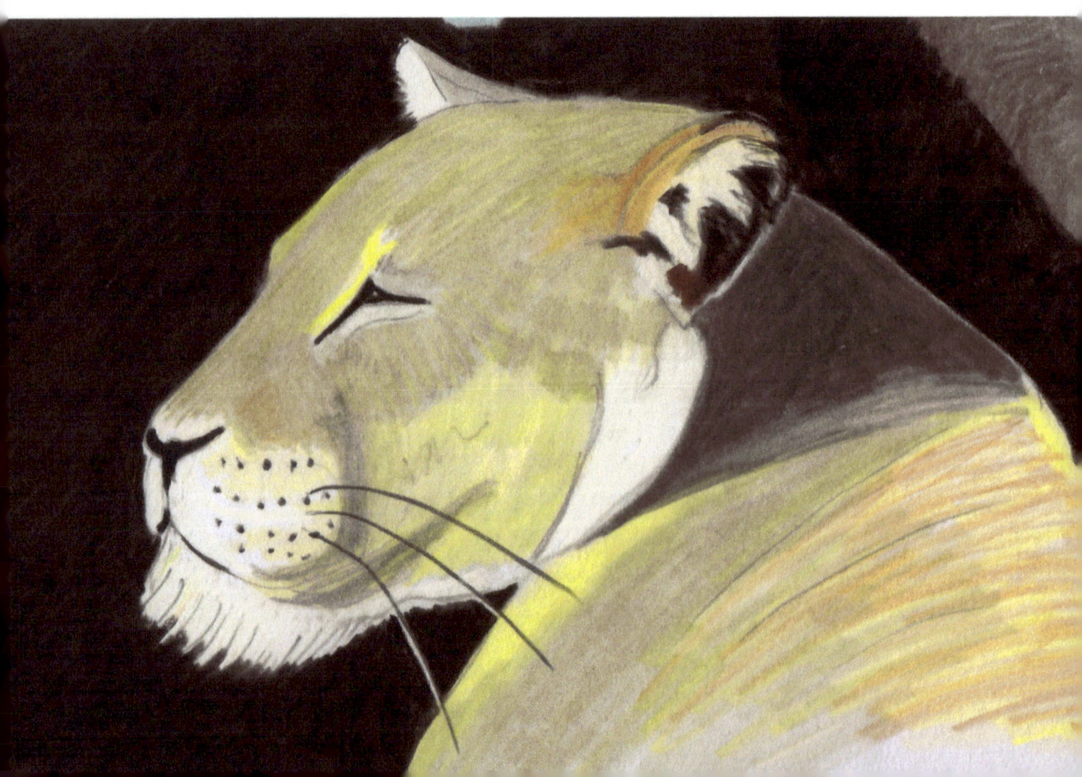

Thursday

At 1pm, I went to the organic supermarket to buy food. Something was wrong with my sense of taste. I bought a strange assortment of grilled chicken leg, blackcurrants, blueberries, vanilla coconut ice cream, melon, lamb mince and strawberry milkshake powder, the brand we had at home when I was a kid. Amazingly, it was still on the market. As a kid, I loved that milkshake powder. While I was standing at the checkout, I tried the blackcurrants. They tasted appalling. Somewhere between rotten and acidic. I threw them in the bin by the checkout.

Back at home, Robyn was still at work and I went through my food items one by one. The blueberries looked great but tasted weird, too. I put them in the fridge, hoping to be able to eat them later. The grilled drumstick and lamb were delicious. I also tried the ice cream and almost immediately felt as if I was going to have diarrhoea. So, no ice-cream. Then I tried the strawberry drink. It tasted chemical. I spat it out and chucked the box in the waste bin. I even tasted the plastic shopping bag (although I did not try to eat it). The taste was sharp and chemical, and very unpleasant.

Intense wave: Power and Relaxation, 3.30pm to 4.30pm
I suddenly felt extremely tired and went to bed. I saw a massive lioness. She roared, she huffed, she drove her teeth into flesh. Ripped it away. She loved the lamb. She loved the chicken. She ate like a lion. Smacking and slurping. How wonderful it tasted!!

Later, I read on the internet about lions. They are the masters of power and relaxation. They only 'work' for four hours a day. Here was a good role model for my burnout at work. Relaxed and powerful. At 5.58pm, the next wave started. When was this ever going to end?

Left above: Hungry Lioness
Left below: Powerful Lioness at Rest

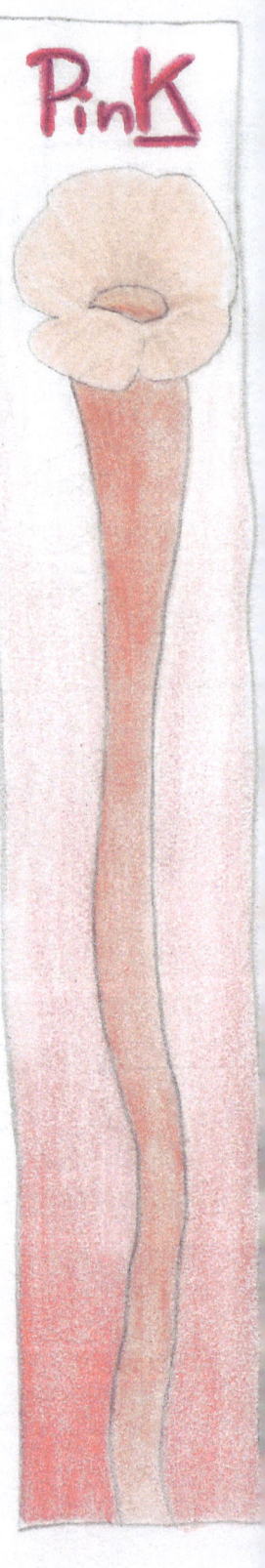

Thursday – Night Waves

I sat upright in bed from midnight to 5.30am, terrified and on edge, thinking about the hole, the worst part, crawling with monsters in its depths. Half-way through the night, I realised that the ugly faces had gone. Somehow, they had disappeared. The hole was plain black now, which was much easier to look at and deal with.

The night-time dialogue consisted of a lot of repetition. It took a lot of patient repeating to get through the wave and convince the monster shape to let go. Here is part of that dialogue:

"The opposite of falling into the hole is not falling into the hole. You can let go of falling into the hole. You don't have to do that. Let go of the idea. Leave it to the River Rhine to take it away, under the bridge, far down the river, where it can dissolve and erode until nothing is left anymore. Let go of it. Letting go, softly, slowly, let go of the idea. You can be beautiful and normal and stable again.

Just let go of it.
Just let it go.
Float down the River Rhine.
The river will take care of it.
You can let go of the negative.
You are a shining soul.
You are a shining soul.
Let go of 'open'.
The opposite of 'open' is 'closed'.
You can let go of 'open'.
You may have always been a bit too open.
Let go of it.
You can drop it.
Let openness flow down the river.
Away.
Dissolving.
Until it is gone.
And a normal boundary emerges.
Let go of the idea and the feeling of openness.
Repairing it.
Repairing. Borders. Normal borders. Restoring. Good borders.
Restoration of normal borders. Boundaries.

Left, from left to right: Screaming Madness; The Black Hole and Pink

"He violated those boundaries with his electric fire stick. Now they can heal. The idea of 'open' can leave, can go away, float away on the River Rhine.

"Too open is not healthy.
Open and close, closed.
There are borders that can open, and there are borders that never open, like the skin.
They can all let go of the idea of permanently open.
Even the vagus nerve can be too open.
It also can let go of the idea of too open.

There were many different aspects in the ayahuasca journey.
A too open hole.
Me almost falling in.
You can let go of too open.
You can let go.
Letting go.
The river takes all the energies away that are connected to the open hole.
It is not any hole.

And the river can dissolve the idea of open, of no boundaries, healing.
Healing a hole.
Healing the hole.
Healing is good.
Healing is very good.

He forced it open.
He made it open.
Permanently open.
You can let go of him now.
You don't need him anymore.
Restoring borders.
Healing.

Closing.
It is time to close.
It is time to close.

It is time to close.
Protect.
Be good to yourself.
Love yourself and close yourself."

This self-monologue went on for hours. In the morning, the black hole suddenly turned pink! When I realised what it was, I started to cry. It was all pink now.
The hole.
No more black.
It was actually a body structure.
Pink was a good colour.
And the inner child suddenly had her face back.

Open and Close

Friday Morning – The End!

I was wrecked after a seventh night without sleep. I was still shaky from the last wave when the next panic wave started.

Robyn got up with me at 6am and we went for a long walk along the river. I calmed down. We talked a lot. Robyn 'saw' or felt a great friendly snake leaving. It was amazing that she could feel her too. I could feel that Mother Ayahuasca had left. It was over. There would be no more 'monsters'. I felt relief.

We walked home. I went into the garden and lay down on the lawn with my sleeping bag. The weather was beautiful, sunny and dry with a big blue sky.

Robyn thought I was okay, so she left for an appointment with her chiropractor. Everything was fine. I drifted away, but did not really fall asleep.

Robyn

A passage from Robyn's diary, Friday, 13 July 2018:

"I'm in some tacky café, charging my phone and whiling away the time until my appointment with the chiropractor, Mr Zabniewski.

"Alison had another bad night, didn't sleep, had to have all the lights on. But at least she could handle me sleeping in the bedroom with the lights off. She woke me before 7am and asked for help. Asked me to go for a walk with her along the river.

"It was good we did that. A bit of normality. I'm feeling very calm and able to give her the stability she needs. It was good to be in the shade of the trees by the water, listening to birdsong. It calmed her down, though sometimes she had to cry. She told me a lot of positive things that happened on her journey with Mother Ayahuasca. She's convinced that the ayahuasca has got rid of a lot of old stuff. Even though it's been hard, literally fighting her demons, she feels like she's been able to let a lot of pain and trauma go. Float away down the River Rhine, which is right next to the building where they did the ayahuasca ceremony. She showed me some photos of it in the early morning light, its surface shining like a golden mirror and with the cream-coloured building opposite reflected in the water. She said she thought that the ayahuasca had healed something in her brain that might've killed her – brain cancer or a tumour? She didn't say. She had to cry after she told me that.

"I gently said that perhaps it was time to thank Mother Ayahuasca for all that she'd done for her and ask her to let her continue her journey without her. Maybe just with me as a guide. That I could take over now. Thanking Mother Ayahuasca made her cry.

"We reached one point where she often stops. There's a tree there with a hole in its trunk at eye-level and she often puts flowers in there or a feather, or a gift of wine. She put a feather back in there that had fallen to the ground.

"I had a vision of Mother Ayahuasca too, while we were standing there, as Alison was touching 'her' tree. I saw Mother Ayahuasca as a big, yellow, kindly snake. So friendly she was, with a big head, that I stroked her almost as if she were a dog. And, somehow, we communicated with each other silently that it was time for her to return to the forest and for me to continue the process as Alison's guide.

"She went back towards the forest but, at the edge, she turned and looked at me, right into my eyes. She looked at me with so much love, and we had a meeting, somehow, an acknowledgment. Mutual recognition. Then she went into the forest.

"Since then, I've been feeling happy. I feel blessed to have had this brief connection with Mother Ayahuasca via Alison. I feel so calm and grown-up, somehow. Confident that we will weather this storm of hers together.

"She's had so many insights. Mother Ayahuasca seems so logical. She's told her that everything, everything in one's life is connected with everything else. Alison found out, for example, that the reason she likes cold things to eat or cold places to visit is because of what happened with that terrible gynaecologist when she was thirteen. He literally burnt her inside. He burnt her with a kind of fire – cauterised something unnecessarily. That's why she doesn't like fire.

"Now I'm wondering whether we should get the wood-burning stove we had planned to instal in the lounge.

"Alison's been writing everything down about her journey. Pages and pages of it. Yesterday, I phoned her from work to ask her something and she said another 'wave' had come, but it was positive this time.

"She felt she really needed to eat meat and went shopping for chicken legs and lamb's mince, which she made into little patties and fried with herbs. Then a lioness came to visit. "The fridge is full of all sorts of stuff. She also made a huge chicken, lentil and spring onion salad but couldn't eat it. I had some for breakfast.

"I'm feeling so good. So happy and calm and able to be there for her. It wasn't good that these people gave her such a high dose. They should do these ayahuasca sacred voyages over at least three days, with only a tiny cup on the first day, then a bigger one on the next, and only on the third day should they give someone the amount that Alison got. It was too much. She could've ended up in the psychiatric clinic. She's still not out of danger. I'm worried about her being on her own. She needs to sleep. She needs to be able to sleep. Lack of sleep can give even normal people psychosis. I need to cleanse our flat with sage smoke, put flowers in every room.

"She wants to give Mother Ayahuasca a big bunch of yellow and white flowers. Yellow gerbera and freesias, white roses and the frothy little white blooms of baby's breath. I saw some yellow tansy and white yarrow and a purple wildflower, that I don't know the name of, growing on a piece of wasteland on the way from the station to this café. Perhaps I'll pick a bunch of them for her on my way home."

Friday Noon – Taking the Fight to a New Level

I was still in the garden at 10.30am when I sat up with a start. A wave of terror was coming. A strong wave. Really strong. I grabbed the grass and tried to sit it out, but it got stronger by the minute. This was becoming an emergency. I ran upstairs and fired up the PC, did a Google search for "psychiatric clinic", found one and called the number. The woman on the other end of the line said, "Oh, you're calling as an emergency. I'll put you through." But she left me on hold for more than 15 minutes. I counted every second. I was hanging on by the skin of my teeth. If this is your way of treating emergencies, I thought, I don't need you. I put the phone down and called a private clinic that I found while waiting on hold. A very friendly person answered the phone. He was great. I didn't know it at the time, but he was the managing director. I told him about my ayahuasca effects and he said: "No problem." I could go there immediately. The staff would be ready for me in half an hour. They specialised in panic attacks (among other problems) and had all the medication needed to help me to sleep after 155 sleepless hours. The clinic was very expensive, but I could manage three days without drawing down my savings. I called Mr Theobald, the taxi driver, packed a small suitcase and, on a whim, added my coloured pencils and a new scrapbook. I wrote a short note to Robyn, and placed it on the floor in the hall. Address, telephone number, why I was going. After twenty minutes, the taxi arrived and we set off to Lintrup Forest, wherever that was.

Emergency Admission

Looking back to this Friday, I have to say that, for once, I got very, very lucky, considering the circumstances.

It was rush hour on Friday and the start of the summer holidays. The car radio announced 270 kilometres of traffic jams on the motorways in the area. It's hard to believe, but, somehow, we avoided them all. The cars in the oncoming lanes were frozen head-to-tail but, after two hours, I arrived at the clinic having managed to stay on top of the panic all that time.

I had never been to a psychiatric clinic, but had watched disturbing movies about them. *One Flew Over the Cuckoo's Nest* came to mind. So, this was a jump into the dark. I prayed, silently, that I wouldn't end up like Jack Nicholson's character. Fortunately, the clinic was more like a four-star hotel, with a lot of 'activities' for the residents. Everybody was relaxed. They even allowed dogs. I love dogs, and there were eleven of them on the premises. The staff were incredibly friendly and I had a wonderful time. As promised, they got me to sleep without a panic attack. I ended up staying for two weeks. During that time, I found out that my poor brain was more rattled than I first thought.

'Medicinology'

The next day, saved from the panic attacks by medication and with a bit of breathing space, I carried out some more internet research on ayahuasca and its impacts on the brain and body. I was interested in the neuroscience of it all. I found out that ayahuasca affects the dopamine balance and the extrapyramidal motor system. I did not copy the links because I was not thinking about writing a book back then. Here is my summary of the different pages:

The dopamine balance is related to the neurobiology of psychoses. Dopaminergic systems are also involved in the regulation of hormonal balance. Dopaminergic neurons are found in the central nervous system, especially in the midbrain, but also in the brain stem. Dopamine is also a neurotransmitter in some systems of the vegetative nervous system and regulates blood flow to the internal organs. It is required for a large number of vital control and regulation processes. Among other things, dopamine influences extrapyramidal motor function, and this may be related to Parkinson's disease. The use of strongly dopaminergic substances can cause similar symptoms to Parkinson's disease in healthy people.

Perhaps this was the cause of my repetitive and violent body movements during that first, lost hour after taking ayahuasca. But ayahuasca does not have to work like that. During the second ceremony, I observed that François moved around elegantly. What I read seemed to provide some evidence that I had taken an overdose of ayahuasca.

Next, I ran a further Google search for information on the 'extrapyramidal motor system' (EPS).

I learned that the extrapyramidal motor system is connected to the cerebellum and the optical reflex centres. It provides harmony of body movement and posture. The EPS strongly influences muscle tone and movement control.

I also read about intrusive thoughts, because I had had a lot of these during the past week. I found out that, in psychotraumatology, intrusion is understood as the remembering and re-experiencing of traumatic events. Intrusions include flashbacks and nightmares. They can also appear as intrusive thoughts and ideas penetrating into consciousness. Intrusions are considered a symptom of post-traumatic stress disorder (PTSD). They are usually triggered by a key stimulus (trigger). People suffering from PTSD often avoid triggering situations. The affected person can relive the traumatic event in great detail. The re-experiencing can include thoughts, images and perceptions. However, the influence on memory is limited. Intrusions can overwhelm a person and repressing the memory is often not possible. The drug Risperidone is often used to reduce intrusions in PTSD patients. Negative intrusive thoughts can trigger panic attacks.

Risperidone was one of the two drugs I had been prescribed since arriving at the clinic.

Two Weeks in a Psychiatric Clinic

My first night in the clinic was the first time I had slept in a week. But, when I woke up, I found out that, despite the medication, the horrible stuff was still there. Just further away.

This was not going to be as easy a fix as I had thought. I had a lot of nightmares and, despite the pills, slept with the lights on. I was very shaky in the morning and remained that way for quite some time. The bad feelings came back again and again. But at least I *could* sleep and that made a big difference. Here are some of the events that I recorded in my journal from the two weeks at the clinic:

Friday, first night at the clinic

I took some pills called Lorazepam and Risperidone. I was drenched in sweat. It looked as if only the tops of the ayahuasca waves came through.
Wave at 10:18pm. I woke up. Screaming?
Read a celebrity soap magazine to get away from the bad stuff.
Next wave: 11.59pm
Next wave: 0.02am
I was really trying to keep my eyes open.
Next wave. 0:18am
Next wave: 0.22am
Heatwave
Next wave: 0.33am
Next wave: 0.43am
After calling for the nurse, I took a second Lorazepam pill. Peace at last!
Fighting continued in my sleep until 6.18am
It felt as if I had fought for half the night.
But the fighting took place in my sleep via nightmares and not while I was awake! This is a great improvement!"
Sunday night
At 11.40pm, I woke up in severe panic. Shit! I took a second
Lorazepam pill. I was frightened.
Kaleidoscope.
Snow globe.

Thursday morning

I slept well! The relaxation technique we were taught yesterday really worked.

I will stay for a second week, despite the costs.

It is very strange: I can draw much better, I can sing much better and more clearly. Is that a side-effect of ayahuasca?

Second Sunday, afternoon

Some parts of my inner being have an authentic, more or less beautiful, shape and some have a form that has been fused with negativity. These parts are frozen in time but although their core is frozen, they still develop by collecting more of the same negativity. It is important to let go of every bit of negativity and to reverse it to its authentic beautiful form. This is possible at every stage of deformation, because the true form never ceases to exist.

The exception is madness. Matter moves. It also moves in the brain. This results in a tiny proportion of mad brains in both animals and humans. Still, if you encounter a mad brain, you are just as fucked as you would be with an asteroid strike or a super volcano. But because of the small proportion of mad brains, the default setting for all beings is trust. Matter is moving, but the space in between crashes is large enough for organisms (at the level of the population) to control and reproduce.

Second Monday

No dreams last night. Interesting dialogue about burnout with the chief physician.

I've finished all the drawings – the documentation of my ayahuasca horror trip and its healing.

The Snake didn't like her yellow-white patchwork. I turned her golden-yellow instead.

So, this is it now. Every picture is finished.

Second Tuesday

My first day without needing to take any pills.

Despite the difficult nights, I had a very good time at the 'clinic hotel'. The food was excellent and – despite my intolerances to fructose, gluten and lactose – they could offer a healthy, beautifully presented and varied diet. The fitness room had a boxing sack. How great was that! And, almost every day, a fitness trainer came to the clinic. The art therapy room was equipped with all kinds of stuff that everyone was allowed to use, and the music therapy room had very big drums, djembes, guitars and didgeridoos, which anyone could use. There were classes on relaxation, and group and private therapy sessions. The town swimming pool was across the road and a kind of zoo was only 150 metres up the road. During my stay at the clinic, I developed a kind of drawing and writing fever. I was almost frantic with energy (and fear) and started to confront (and heal) all of my demons, starting with the least severe. I drew and drew and drew. Sometimes, I drew seven pictures in one day. I needed to get it all out. I needed to be able to let go of it. It needed a manageable size and form for that. Like a book. It was going to be a book. With pictures. In cartoon book style.

I drew and drew and worked my two black coloured pencils down to their stubs. At the end of the two weeks, the new scrapbook I had been given for my birthday was full. Not a single empty page remained.

Healing the Horror – The Story in Pictures

I spent the first week after the ceremony in a sleepless seven-night-and-day panic, stumbling from one surfacing monster to the next, trying to talk them out of their monster shape and into their authentic shape. It brought me to the very brink of psychosis. Talking is a weak tool when it comes to the subconscious. The subconscious mind is impressed by colours, by pictures, by emotions and by real-life occurrences with an emotional content, but it generally ignores words and logical reasoning. My subconscious, at least, is not very much impressed by words. It's very hard to make a dent in the subconscious by talking or writing alone, which are primarily left-brain activities.

When I went to the clinic six days after taking the ayahuasca, the surfacing of monsters was stopped by medication and I could finally sleep. I was diagnosed with a hallucinogenic-induced fear disorder and PTSD. During the first few nights, I had nightmares, but I couldn't remember them when I woke up. The process was ongoing but, luckily, without my conscious involvement. I had space to breathe again, although the fear and panic immediately returned at night when I tried to skip the medication. It took two weeks to manage a night free of pills.

On 17 July, ten days after the ayahuasca ceremony, I started to draw. This was finally when healing occurred. Drawing with coloured pencils is a process that requires you to constantly choose form and colour. This keeps the subconscious involved. Coloured pencils also have very tiny tips, so it takes some time to fill in blocks of colour. A postcard-sized drawing could keep my subconscious engaged for over two hours.

In my experience, it is very difficult to keep the subconscious interested in one particular subject over a long period of time, but drawing with coloured pencils is one method. (Ritual is another method that can sometimes take days to create and complete.) If you apply the subconscious to the task of a 'healing picture' and contrast it with the 'not yet healed' picture afterwards, the subconscious can take the new picture on board as the new and correct form. You can't do it the other way around, because this would complete the monster first, which would then stand alone for the amount of time needed to draw the healing picture. This was a sure panic trigger for me. Of course, the subject matter in itself is also a trigger, bringing back all the difficult emotions attached to it. So, I had to maintain a balance between triggering another panic attack and starting to truly heal the monsters.

What does a healed monster look like? A healed monster is one that has lost its negative emotional content. Even five weeks later, some pictures still carried a residue of negative emotions (especially the first 'Anger' and 'Madness' pictures), but most had turned into harmless 'illustrations.' The sequence of the story in pictures was difficult to reconstruct, because healing took place in reverse order. The problematic topics began with the most severe on 7 of July and progressed to less severe topics on 13 July. But the healing started on 17 July with the *least* severe topics and progressed backwards to the most severe topics on 24 July. In that way, the first and worst topics were healed last, because it took a lot of groundwork and courage (and sometimes medication) to face them again.

At the clinic, I painted thirteen monster pictures and nineteen healing pictures. Sometimes, the shadow and its solution were present in the same picture, such as the Fire and Pain picture with the water bottle. Sometimes, several problematic topics appeared in the same picture, so one picture required different solutions, such as the Demon Queen picture, with the two problems of Evil and Power. The healing pictures for Power consisted of the two lionesses, and the healing pictures for Evil were the blue Matter Moving picture and the Truth is *One* and Shining Soul pictures. The very first picture I drew was Screw Top, where I screwed my own head off. I still don't understand what that was about.

I managed to pair the topics up reasonably well in chronological order. The table on the next page provides an overview. It shows the dates on which the topics occurred. Most occurred in the very first wave, but quite a few also came in later waves.

The table also shows the dates when these topics were painted. Thank

Table of the Healing Process

Problematic Shape			Authentic Healed Shape		
Date of first occurrence	Pair No. and Title	Date of drawing	Date of first occurrence	Pair No. and Title	Date of drawing
7.7. 10:00	1.1 Evil	22.7.	7.7. 23:00	1.2 Matter Moving	21.7.
			7.7. 23:00	1.3 Truth is ONE	21.7.
			7.7. 23:00	1.4 Shining Soul	21.7.
7.7. 10:00	2.1 Power	22.7.	18.7.	2.2 Lioness B	18.7.
			17.7.	2.3 Lioness A	17.7.
7.7. 10:00	3.1 The Hole	17.7.	13.7. 5:00	3.2 Pink	17.7.
			13.7. 5:00	3.3 Open and Close	24.7.
7.7. 10:00	4.1 Madness	22.7. 19:00	22.7. 17:00	4.2 Sadness	22.7. 17:00
			7.7. 23:00	4.3 Trust	22.7. 6:00
7.7. 10:00	5.1 Deadly Anger	20.7.	20.7.	5.2 Livid Anger	20.7.
7.7. 10:00	6.1 Fire	21.7.			
8.7. 24:00	6.1 Pain	21.7.	8.7. 24:00	6.2 Water	21.7.
8.7.	7.1 Go away!	19.7.	8.7. 24:00	7.2. Letting Go	19.7.
9.7. 5:00	8.1 Burnt Corpse	20.7.	9.7. 5:00	8.2 Little Girl age 13	23.7.
				8.3 Healing	20.7.
9.7. 5:00	9.1 Face/Deformation	20.7.	20.7.	9.2 Authenticity and Beauty	20.7.
10.7.	10.1 Mechanical Man	20.7.	10.7. 5:00	10.2 Desperation – The River is a Healer	17.7.
10.7.	11.1 Screw Top	17.7.			
11.7.	12.1 Death	18.7.	11.7.	12.2 Water is Life	22.7
7.7. 10:00	13.1 Start	23.7.	19.7.	13.2 The End	19.7.
			22.7.	13.3 Thank You	22.7.
28.7.	14.1 Fear	30.7.	30.7.	14.2 Healing Ritual	30.7.
			30.7.	14.2 Trust II	30.7.

goodness I found such a good clinic that gave me the space to heal.

Creating this 'bound' book (almost like 'spellbinding'), with a beautiful front and back cover, has also been part of the healing process.

Formatting and rewriting the different versions of this book also gave me back some control over the topics after I was ready to withstand the triggers. A book is much easier to handle than phantoms in your head.

'Madness' was a really difficult monster. The fear of losing my mind was so terrifying that I could hardly touch the topic. Painting it helped, but did not resolve it entirely. I finally found a way to express and release it by dancing. I chose two pieces of music, one very short piece with a lot of drums and one longer soothing song. Then, one morning, I allowed Madness to take over my body and express itself for one minute and 33 seconds (the duration of the first piece of music). The first time I let Madness take over I was very afraid because I wasn't at all sure if would be able to step out of it again. But, despite my fear, it worked very well. After one week, the fear of going mad subsided and, after a second week, it was gone.

At home again, on 28, 29 and 30 July, one final topic appeared – Fear – and was healed by a ritual and the drawing of an additional picture. Whether I have managed to heal everything, I can't say. Three times already, I have thought "This is the end". Nevertheless, Fear is the final topic in this book.

Recipe for a Personal Healing Ritual

Fear was in a category of its own. It felt like an out-of-control looming dark spirit that seized me again and again out of nowhere, not in the form of a monster shape but as pure panic energy. It was larger than me. I knew I would need a long and elaborate balancing counter-measure if I was to make it leave me. I was afraid I would never be able to heal it. Still, I had to try. I couldn't go on like that. So, I started to plan a beautiful and respectful long ritual, something to impress my subconscious, my emotions and these out-of-control energies.

If you are planning a ritual, let all the elements come to you via your subconscious mind. This may take some time. Where should it take place, at what time of the day? How is it going to start? How is it going to end? What will happen in between? Which items are needed and what will you do with them? How are you going to symbolise your current state of being, your problem? How are you going to symbolise the dissolving of the problem? What will you do to help it heal? What will you say, sing or do? If you ask your subconscious whether your problem is best symbolised by red or blue, soft or hard, cold or hot, you will get an answer from inside. You can balance this with the opposite to those answers.

It might be that some of the details will only come to you during the ritual itself. As the problem is very real, you have to do something equally real. You cannot fake it or 'play' it. You have to truly mean it, otherwise nothing is going to happen. In that respect, the ritual is a sacred way to create a new reality. Because of that, I won't tell you exactly what I did. But I will give you some ideas to consider:

Step 1: Planning

- Choose a colour scheme appropriate to your problem (in my case, black, yellow and white).
- Choose a time that feels appropriate to you
- (in my case, darkness becoming light, sunrise, 5.49am).
- Choose a site in nature that feels appropriate to you
- (in my case, a river bank).
- Involve the forces and spirits of nature: water, fire, air, soil, a tree, a river, a cave, a glade, a hilltop or any other forces that seem appropriate to you. Be respectful.
- Choose border markers that are appropriate to you
(in my case, white swan feathers attached to a stick and a white-and-yellow line on the ground. The line was made from white flour and turmeric powder. Use only natural ingredients that do not harm nature).
- Choose a gift appropriate to your problem
(The gift should be dear to you. It should be beautiful and unique and can be expensive. Look around your home. The minute one part of you thinks, "Oh no…", you have found your gift. Keep in mind, on an emotional level, your ritual will be just as strong as your gift. If you chose a 'weak' gift, no healing will occur).
- Choose the other ingredients to make your ritual beautiful and meaningful. Ideas for this might pop into your mind over a period of one or two days. Create your own personal choreography. (In my case, these ingredients were towels and blankets in yellow and white (and an occasional lilac); black flowerbed compost from a plastic bag; yellow and white body paint; yellow rose petals; white candles; a portable CD player; two CDs with appropriate tracks (one was the prayer *Thank the Water* by Agnes Baker Pilgrim and the other was Te-Kah's song from

Left: *Looming, Almost Uncontrollable Fear*
Above: *Healing Ritual for Panic*
(If you want to impress your subconscious, don't be stingy! Give it the whole works.)

the Disney movie *Moana*, in which the protagonist talks to the fiery lava monster Te-Kah, places the Heart of Te-Fiti, a sacred stone, in the centre of an ammonite structure on the monster's breast, which causes it to turn into its authentic form, Te-Fiti, a beautiful green goddess who holds the power to create life.))
- You will probably also need a broom and rubbish bags to clean up the ritual site before and after your ceremony.
- You might want to bring a partner along to guard you during your ritual. Or, you might prefer to undertake the ritual on your own in order to be more scared and, therefore, more 'emotionally involved'. But of course this is at your own risk. In a densely populated area I recommend bringing a partner along for reasons of safety, especially if in the dark. At the end of my ritual, I had an 'intruder'. However, when he saw my yellow-and-white body paint, he smiled knowingly and retreated, which I appreciated.

Step 2: Preparation
- Buy or collect the necessary materials.
- Visit your chosen site the afternoon before your ritual. On closer inspection, do you think it is appropriate for your ritual? If not, choose a different site. I found that I had to do this.
- Clean the chosen site and its surroundings of rubbish.

Step 3: Ritual
- Inspect the site. Is everything still in order?
- Mark your boundaries.
- Place all your ritual materials inside the boundary.
- Make your place beautiful.
- Start with a prayer.
- Follow your own choreography to turn darkness/negativity into light/authenticity, or follow whatever kind of healing process you have chosen.
- End by saying 'Thank You' to the forces of nature and the healing forces.
- Pack everything away.

Step 4: Cleaning and Closing
- Clean the site and remove the boundaries with your brush or broom so that no trace remains.

Left: Trust II

If you want to 'im-press' and 'rewrite' your subconscious mind, don't be stingy. Use all levels of involvement at your disposal: colour, setting, emotion, real life activity, beauty. Involve and thank the forces of nature. Then, hopefully, it will work as well for you as it did for me.

Last Insight (for now)

It was 31st of July, the last day of this terrifying month. What was my reason again for participating in the ayahuasca ceremony? To search for healing for my burnout syndrome.

But what was behind my burnout? It was my constant running. I have been running, running, running all my life. I have twisted my ankles many, many times in this process of 'running'. When I am stressed, I want to go fast, faster, faster. This is the opposite of Robyn, who slows down when she's stressed. As a workaholic in the workplace, I have always gone fast. Before that, I was always extremely stressed as a student. And my mum tells me I started to run almost before I could walk.

As a little kid, I started to walk upright by carrying around, and using as support, a lime-green plastic waste-paper basket. I walked on tiptoe most of the time. When I had mastered that, I started to run and never stopped. My mum says that every time someone opened the door, I shot out and many times I fell immediately. But that didn't faze me. I always had patches on my knees from regularly ripping my woollen tights. She says I tore myself loose most of the times we went walking together and she always had to chase me through gardens and around corners. I was a constant runner.

Before I could walk and run, however, I was a so-called cry-baby. My mum tells me I was extremely nervous and frequently woke up with a start, looking scared. I was easily woken by noises and I cried a lot. Sometimes, she felt quite desperate because of that. She thought the chain-smoking Mr Smith, with whom she had shared a tiny office while she was pregnant with me, was to blame for that. She thought the second-hand smoke had affected my health while I was still in her womb.

Therefore, it came as a major revelation to suddenly realise that the energy behind my running and constant stress was fear. It was panic. All my life I had been running from this energy inside of me. It formed a ball in my tummy. I couldn't eat. I just had to go fast, at whatever I was doing.

I called my mum to find out what could have frightened me so much as a baby that it could have had such a lasting effect. She said I had been like that "right from the start", which, in my case, meant ten days after birth. In the 1960s, I had spent the first ten days of my life in the baby ward of the maternity hospital while my mum spent her time recovering in the mother's ward. The standard time was five days but my mum had to stay a bit longer because of a perineal section. Back then, mothers were given their babies only for feeding and at fixed times of the day. What happened to me during those ten days remains unclear. But fear and panic have been in me all my life. They remained in me even after fifty years and they were huge. Now that they had surfaced, they were so huge that I had needed medication to deal with them.

Some people think birth itself is a trauma. Well, I know this is untrue because, when I was thirty-five years old, my birth came back to me in a Gestalt therapy session while I was training to become a Gestalt therapist. It was amazing and ecstatic and weird. All my senses shifted. Noise didn't mean much anymore because I already knew noise as an unborn child. It was something in the background most of the time that wasn't 'doing' anything. Vision didn't mean much anymore. It was new and wasn't working properly at the very beginning. But my skin became an immense tactile organ and I could feel so much more. Birth is a natural process and it is meant to be beautiful. Your babies will not react to voice or vision, but they are tactile superheroes. My rebirth experience went like this:

Suddenly there is something like a 'hard surface' which is a completely new experience. I experience gravity for the first time – I can't lift or move my head anymore! It is suddenly too heavy. This is new, and kind of funny. Suddenly, there is this new thing, air, and it is incredibly smooth. I can feel every wisp of air flowing past my cheek. I can feel every single hair on my skin. It's amazing. It's beautiful. I am totally ecstatic. A whole world of new feelings! Everything new and beautiful.

So, I was quite sure that my birth was not the trauma I was looking for, although, according to what my mum told me, my actual birth was different from the ideal one I had experienced in the Gestalt therapy session. But something happened at that hospital that frightened me so much that fear became a cornerstone of my being. It was a major reason for my success, too, because I needed to be really busy and fast all the time, all my life.

It looked like I had found the reason behind my burnout syndrome after all.

A fear, an 'open Gestalt', that got stuck in me during my first ten days in the world.

I let go of fear during the ritual. The river took most of the energy away, flowing downstream with it, allowing it to dissolve. Healing it.

I hoped that the Gestalt therapist that the clinic had found for me could help me with what remained to be integrated. I hoped I would be able to talk what remained of my *fear* out of its negativity and into its authentic form, which is *inner peace* and *trust*.

Three days after the ritual, I returned to the ritual site to sit on the river bank. Beside the site were three large rocks in the middle of the river. At normal water levels, they couldn't be reached, but, due to a nine-week heatwave, the water table was at a record low, lower now than on the Sunday morning when I had conducted the ritual. I could reach the rocks by balancing on smaller ones without having to wade through the water. When I reached the rocks, I sat on one for a while. I noticed that there was a structure on the surface of the neighbouring rock. Looking at it for some time, I realised it was an impression, a large ammonite the size of my hand.

Large ammonite structure, its centre filled with water.

I had never found fossils on these rocks before, even though I had been to the river many times and there were rocks and stones all over the place. The rock here was not even a fossil-rich rock, such as chalk, but greywacke, a very hard type of old sandstone.

I was amazed, because it reminded me very much of the ammonite structure on the breast of the lava monster Te-Kah, in the movie *Moana*, whose song I had played during the ritual. In the film, the ammonite structure is central to the healing of the monster. The structure on the stone looked very much like that in the film. I filled the centre of the ammonite impression with water. If you've seen the film, you'll be struck by the resemblance between 'my' ammonite and Te-Kah's 'heart'. The nautilus shells I had drawn in my healing journey sketchbook are close relatives to ammonites.

Yenna had said that taking ayahuasca is like someone shaking the snow globe that is you. It will take some time for the snow to settle. But then a new picture can emerge.

Snow Globe – The End – Me and My Thirteen-year-old Girl

Thank You, Mother Ayahuasca

Thank you, Mother Ayahuasca, big friendly snake.
Thank you for all that you showed me.
Thank you for healing that thing in my head.
Thank you for totally and immediately stopping my hair loss.
Thank you for making my digestion so much better.
Thank you for substantially improving my leg and my ankle.
Thank you for giving me all these insights.

And thank you for showing yourself to Robyn on that Friday morning. When she described her encounter to me, stroking your big head like a dog, I knew immediately that this was real on some level. Because, in her unusual description of a snake encounter, I immediately recognised my own feelings that I had kept secret from her.

But your power to stir up unresolved mess is not without danger.

You poured an incredible amount of darkness into my life in one go. And I couldn't handle that. I probably would have been better without drug-induced PTSD in my life. There is much to learn and integrate. I do not know if any of the dark stuff has really gone or just moved back into its depths. The panic attacks are fading, becoming less and less intense. Nevertheless, I thank you for helping me to try to make sense of it all.

Thank you!

Left: Mother Ayahuasca

Ayahuasca Horror Trip – Why Me?

Yenna told me that, in her experience, ayahuasca horror trips are rare. At the wellness centre in Duisburg, they see about three really bad trips in every 500 ayahuasca journeys. She said she wouldn't volunteer if they were more common. She had only experienced a bad trip two or three times in her five years working as a guide.

My horror trip felt like an overdose, even though I only drank one cup of ayahuasca like everybody else. Some of the others drank three cups on their first voyage. Although there are many positive reports and books about taking ayahuasca, many of the participants of my group had negative experiences. I found out that the painting of the very large black skull island that hung on the wall in the main room of the wellness centre had been painted by the centre's founder. He must have had at least one really bad trip to have painted that. But everyone else in my group went on a second journey. Nobody else had a trip like mine that lasted for almost seven months. Perhaps it happened because I was given the last of 25 cups and the particles of the tea, which contain much higher quantities of the drug than the watery solution, had already settled at the bottom. This seems like a sound explanation for an overdose.

In the book, *Ayahuasca: A near-death transformation,* Adriano Lucca writes about his own ayahuasca horror trip [9]. He describes a series of consecutive nightmarish journeys in a Huni Kuin village in the Amazon rainforest. He writes: "Some first-time consumers of ayahuasca have a beautiful and powerful experience. I found them to be a small minority. Others seem to 'need' to go through a hellish but very transformative experience. I was one of them. I wrote this book so they can better prepare themselves."

When I discovered the drug-induced trap door in my psyche leading to the hellish 'essence of evil', I had questions similar to Lucca's: "Why me? Am I a bad person? Am I an evil soul of some sort? Have I lost forever the person that I was?" I felt contaminated. It felt as if the 'Forces of Light' had told me personally: "Thou art weighed in the balances and art found wanting." I lost my naïve trust in the essential goodness of the world. I had come to believe in a Great Spirit. Now I was no longer sure if I was part of that. I suddenly felt like an outcast. Not worthy of 'the light'. Even though the snake had told me that The Truth is One, her words could not erase the powerful feelings of meeting evil demonic forces within myself. I had come for spiritual renewal and left with more doubts than ever.

A Note to the Guides: Don't Push the River

Yenna, if I understood her correctly, referred to the organisations brew as a "therapeutic brew." I understood this to mean that this brew was more likely to provide a problem-solving experience than an 'easy brew' which causes only vomiting. This was consistent with the fact that of the twenty-five participants that weekend, many of them first-timers, almost half encountered negative emotions during their first voyage on Saturday. It was also strange that, for a drug known to induce vomiting, no one in the group did so. Gülay experienced severe physical pain; Alexa was gripped by total paralysis of the body so that she couldn't call to the guides when she needed them; Howard and others said they experienced fear or terrifying emotions. Given that none of these experiences deterred the voyagers from the second ceremony, these negative experiences must not have been as intense as mine.

On the positive side, there was one voyager who laughed his head off for two hours, one who spent his time singing softly, and one who engaged in some strange but relaxed and beautiful 'yoga' for several hours.

I was the unlucky one who had an ayahuasca horror trip. To me, it felt like I had been given an overdose, perhaps ten times too much. Nobody wants a participant in severe psychosis or even a death on the premises so, from my own horror trip experience, I recommend the following to the guides in general:

1. Buy a laboratory-style magnetic mixer and keep the jug(s) of ayahuasca stirred at all times during the pouring of the cups to ensure that every cup contains the same amount of sediment. Pour the cups in the kitchen, rather than during the ceremony, and carry the brew into the room in full cups on trays, rather than in jugs. Otherwise, you will distribute a whole range of doses, with everyone consuming different amounts, leading to experiences ranging from 'normal' at the beginning to nothing in the middle to extreme at the end.
2. Have a qualified doctor who is trained as a guide on the premises and stock an anti-psychotic medication, such as Risperidone, and an anti-panic medication, such as Lorazepam, in case of emergency. Given the eight-hour time frame, there is no need to rush. At first, serve only one small gulp. Serve less to smaller-bodied participants. Wait half an hour. Then proceed.
3. Beforehand, ask participants about their diets. Take extra care with

people on strict and long-standing diets because the lack of a normal amount of ayahuasca-inhibitors in the blood may result in more extreme effects.
4. Do *not* decorate the sacred space with pictures of darkness and death or with any terrifying or disturbing images. Remove all negativity from the sacred space. The truth is *one*. The sacred space should reflect that.
5. Do not play dissonant or disturbing music during the ceremony. Don't push the river. Healing will take place at its own pace. Do not try to force healing upon people with the idea of creating a therapeutic set-up. Let it evolve in its own way. Allow Mother Ayahuasca to work in her own way. Create the space, but don't try to fill it with your ideas.
6. Refrain from the 'patriarchal thinking' that only a really bad experience is a 'good' experience; that 'only if I have to fight and be really tough will I receive healing and enlightenment'.

In *Wizard of the Upper Amazon: The story of Manuel Córdova-Rios* (1907), F. Bruce Lamb provides perhaps the earliest Western description of taking ayahuasca and reports only slightly negative dreams after taking ayahuasca for the first time [10]. On page 27, Lamb describes a journey in its native Amerindian Huni Kuin setting to include:
- fasting and a special diet
- red face paint
- a brilliantly illuminated glade in the forest like a cathedral
- an extremely calm environment
- soft chanting (mentioned several times)
- incense burning and cleaning everyone with smoke
- small palm-nut cups filled with liquid
- harmonious singing, one with high falsetto voice of tremulous character (tremolo)

Córdova-Rios explained to Lamb that, to obtain the desired visions, the brew had to be boiled slowly in a special earthenware pot over a low fire and not in an aluminium pot. He warned that taking improperly prepared ayahuasca could be dangerous. Not a single horror trip is mentioned in the entire book.

Left: Picture Detail of Skull Island –
A Desolate Place. One of the Pictures on the Walls of the Main Room

Recommendations for Travellers

I will never go on an ayahuasca journey again. I can't recommend it. But if you think you must take an ayahuasca trip, here are some things to consider:

- Read Adriano Lucca's book (see literature [9]).
- Never travel without guides. Even if you have had positive experiences in the past, Mother Ayahuasca might surprise you in an unwanted way. One of the guides said that Mother Ayahuasca is unpredictable.
- Start with small amounts. Sip a bit of the tea and wait. I recommend choosing an organisation that offers two or three ceremonies over a weekend. These will give you the time to slowly increase the dosage without the pressure of feeling you might miss the experience you have paid for. The ceremonies that I participated in and observed were of eight hours duration. There is no need to hurry.
- Closely observe the team to see if they continuously stir the jug(s) of ayahuasca tea before and while they pour it into individual cups. Watch out for the cups filled from the bottom of the jug. They may contain more sediment and, thus, a significantly higher dose of the drug. Be careful if your cup contains a lot of sediment.
- Prepare your mind. Avoid all negativity during the week before you take the journey. Avoid books, TV, YouTube, the cinema and anything else that might surprise you with negative content. Be good to yourself during that week.
- If the room where the ceremony takes place is decorated with negative pictures, ask yourself if you want to travel with this team at all.
- If you tumble into psychosis, as I almost did, the anti-psychotic drug Risperidone may help. If you start to experience frequent flashes of panic, the anti-panic drug Lorazepam may help you sleep. Both are prescription drugs. Discuss this with your doctor!
- I recommend that you investigate about possible helpers in advance, such as doctors or the nearest psychiatric clinic, just in case you get into trouble.
- Adriano Lucca writes: "If an evil-looking entity emerges, look straight into its eyes. Even if it looks monstrous, it could be beneficial. If you are scared it will feed on your fear to become even more terrifying."
- In advance of the ceremony, think of strong allies that you can visualise who might help you during your trip. Iris Disse published a report of a similar trip in *Psychology*, in which she described successfully fighting against an evil

spirit (her guide!) who wanted to eat and destroy her soul. She got out with the help of her Yoga goddess, Durga.

- There are different brews of 'ayahuasca tea' [11]. The mash of the liana is always mixed with at least one other plant. The different indigenous cultures in the Amazon rainforest and beyond have developed different traditions to work with the plant. The preparation of the drug can sometimes be inadequate, causing intestinal cramps and diarrhoea. Some brews have a pleasant taste with a light aftertaste of orange and sweet alcohol, while others have a bitter taste. Some trigger a cleansing effect (vomiting), others trigger trips, some cause light visions, others are used in so-called 'cura' ceremonies [11], which offer participants "the opportunity to do deep work on themselves", as Lucca puts it [9], meaning often difficult or even terrifying experiences. In other words, there is not only one 'ayahuasca'.

Clinic Painting (Art Therapy): Borders

Two Years Later

It is now more than two years since that weekend. The parade of monsters continued for seven months. After my first ayahuasca ceremony, I was diagnosed with PTSD, and I experienced occasional and disturbing panic flashbacks for quite some time until I performed the *fear*-ritual. I was glad I had a very good Gestalt therapist at my side. The nightmarish experience slowly faded. Unfortunately, I continue to be the same workaholic I was before.

However, my health has improved, my digestion is better and I no longer experience hair loss. My legs and ankle are considerably improved and I am back on my feet again, so to speak. My brain-fog burnout feelings have vanished, too, although I believe this is due to supplements I now take, as recommended in a book by the physician and herbalist, Aviva Romm [12].

My knowledge about my own biography has greatly increased, although I have been unable to resolve the questions concerning my first ten days of life, despite the help from my mum. I have ordered a baby and parenting book that was in wide circulation in the 1960s, to see if I can find any clues about what might have been standard maternity hospital procedures back then.

The experience has also put a great strain on Robyn as, without noticing it myself, I became stubborn, inflexible and aggressive for quite some time.

Drawing and painting have been a source of fun and relaxation, and a steady therapeutic tool throughout my life but, since I finished the last drawing for this book, I have stopped drawing and painting altogether. I simply don't feel like it anymore.

Johann Hari, in his excellent book, *Lost Connections*, describes a scientific experiment conducted with terminally ill patients, who were given large doses of the psychoactive drug psilocybin [13]. Seventy-five per cent of participants had 'heavenly' experiences that changed their lives for the better. Around twenty-five per cent had at least some moments of real terror and for a handful of these it was a horrible six hours [13]. I conclude that taking ayahuasca for the first time is a matter of statistics. Would I do it again? Never.

Left: Smooth Paddling Instead of Frantic Paddling.
Moving Forward with Little Effort Instead of Constant Running.

Two Childhood Traumas and their Resolutions

The drug brought two childhood traumas to the fore: one directly after my birth and one at the age of thirteen. The cause of the first trauma is unknown. It manifested at the physical and mental level in:

- an extremely nervous baby unable to sleep
- a constantly crying fearful baby
- a very stressed mum
- a very skinny child that had to 'run' all the time
- a very athletic older child
- an adult who is 'running' all the time, with an excess of energy
- an adult who feeds on stress, a workaholic with burnout-problems
- major problems with digestion (many intolerances)
- a very successful adult.

The cause of the second childhood trauma was an extremely painful cervical cauterisation process done without anaesthetic. It manifested at the physical and mental level in:

- almost immediately 'forgetting' the incident because I didn't want to 'touch' it or think about it for even a nanosecond
- the inability to have an orgasm, which lasted for decades
- the inability to engage in a relationship prior to the age of forty
- incredibly painful and almost unbearable menstrual cramps
- severe back-pain
- all-male torture fantasies (soldiers, spies, etc.) for two decades
- self-harm practices involving burning matches, taking pride in my self-control right down to the contraction of the pupil of the eye (I did to myself what was done to me, perhaps to achieve some kind of agency or sense of control. At the time, I had no idea why I was doing these things. I stopped the practice soon after I began, because burn scars are lasting 'adornments')
- a loss of self-confidence
- becoming a bit of a recluse
- suicidal depression at the age of twenty-one.

I thought I had resolved all but one of these issues during my five-year training to become a Gestalt therapist.

The subconscious translated these traumas into 'fitting' images, which took the shape of monsters and uncontrollable emotions of fear and panic. The drug brought these monsters unfiltered to the fore, causing PTSD with severe panic attacks, intrusive thoughts and unwanted but uncontrollable mental pictures.

After I had come to understand the principle behind the formation of the monsters (every monster, no matter how terrifying, was a warped shape of something positive), I resolved them and the associated panic and fear with intense, ten-hour-a-day, self-therapy (art, ritual, writing) and twenty sessions of Gestalt therapy. During the two weeks at the clinic, I had to support the process with the anti-psychotic drug Risperidone and the anti-panic drug Lorazepam. I kept those drugs around for a while, just in case, but I didn't need to take them again after about four weeks.

After one year, the ayahuasca-induced PTSD vanished completely. am positive that the therapy approach taken in this book will work for many childhood traumas. Trauma leaves a deep impression in the subconscious mind. To overwrite or heal this impression you need an equally impressive event. As long as you are not hurting anyone there are no limits to fantasy. I recommend self-therapy with art, writing and ritual, regardless of whether the PTSD is drug-induced or not. Ayahuasca should be avoided.

During the second year, I started to take a lot of supplements, including zinc, iron, vitamin C and vitamin D [12], and even started a ketogenic diet after concluding that my burn-out brain-fog problems might be the effect of a type-3 brain-centred 'diabetes' [14]. After taking the supplements, my stress levels have reduced considerably. I have much more energy and have even started to do sports again. I am still a workaholic, but I am better able to control my running impulses. I have started to eat properly while at work. Thanks to the keto diet, my sleep has greatly improved. Am I healed? Has ayahuasca healed me? The drug put a mountain of stuff on my plate that almost choked me. Almost tumbling into psychosis was no fun at all.

Because the dose of the drug was not properly controlled, I am lucky that I managed to stay on top of it at all. Others may have been less lucky, but you are unlikely to read about them, because they will never be able to write a book. They are locked away in psychiatric institutions.

Literature

[1] Law&Crime Network (18.01.2018): *Larry Nassar Sentencing, Hearing Day 2 Part 1, Victim Impact Statements. (Accessed on YouTube 20.02.2021)* https://www.youtube.com/watch?v=sGsmB8tkS4E

[2] Ogg, Mary J.: *Surgical Smoke Inhalation: Dangerous Consequences for the Surgical Team.* In: NIOSH Science blog. June 18, 2020, MSN, RN, CNOR; *https://blogs.cdc.gov/niosh-science-blog/2020/06/18/surgical-smoke/ (accessed 23.01.2022)*
(Quote: "During surgical procedures, smoke is produced when energy generating devices such as lasers or electrosurgical units also known as cautery are used to stop bleeding or incise tissue. The energy generating devices raise the intracellular temperature to boiling (i.e., 100° C /212° F). At these high temperatures the tissue vaporizes producing surgical smoke. The smoke is often not visible and has an unpleasant odor. The smoke may contain ultra-fine particles, toxic compounds (e.g., benzene, toluene, hydrogen cyanide), viruses (e.g., human papilloma virus [HPV]), and cancer cells (Guideline for Surgical Smoke Safety).")

[3] *WHO guidelines for screening and treatment of precancerous lesions for cervical cancer prevention* (2013). Chapter 5: Screening and treatment of cervical pre-cancer, p. 157.
http://www.who.int/reproductivehealth/publications/cancers/screening_and_treatment_of_precancerous_lesions/en/ (accessed 13.12.2019), (Quote: "10. Inject 3–5 ml of local anaesthetic... Select the appropriate electrode to enable removal of the entire abnormal area in a single pass: for small, low-grade lesions in nulliparous women, use an electrode 1.5 cm wide by 0.5 cm deep; for larger lesions and multiparous women, use an electrode 2.0 cm wide by 0.8 cm deep.
Turn the vacuum suction on and activate the generator.
Excise the lesion: push the electrode perpendicularly into the tissue to a depth of 4–5 mm and draw it laterally across the cervix to the other side, producing a dome-shaped circle of tissue with the canal in the centre...
Note: In some cases, the patient may have a vasovagal reaction, with fainting and plummeting blood pressure. If this happens, stop the treatment immediately and raise the patient's legs as much as possible.")
-> This page of the World Health Organization is no longer available.

But the WHO has published the recommendations as a book: *WHO guidelines for screening and treatment of precancerous lesions for cervical cancer prevention (2013).* *https://www.who.int/reproductivehealth/publications/cancers/screening_and_treatment_of_precancerous_lesions/en/ (accessed 23.01.2022)*

[4] Sato, Joao, R. et. al: *Identification of psychopathic individuals using pattern classification of MRI images.* In: ResearchGate: May 2011, Social Neuroscience. No.6 (5-6), pp. 627-39, Source PubMed; *https://www.researchgate.net/publication/51144740_Identification_of_psychopathic_individuals_using_pattern_classification_of_MRI_images (accessed 23.01.2022)*

[5] Stromberg: Joseph: *The Neuroscientist who discovered he was a psychopath.* *https://www.smithsonianmag.com/science-nature/the-neuroscientist-who-discovered-he-was-a-psychopath-180947814/ (accessed 23.01.2022)*

[6] Wikipedia: *Loop electrical excision procedure.* *https://en.wikipedia.org/wiki/Loop_electrical_excision_procedure (accessed 23.01.2022)* (Quote: "LEEP has many advantages including low cost, high success rate,.[1] The procedure can be done in an office setting and usually only requires a local anaesthetic, though sometimes IV sedation or a general anaesthetic is used.[2]")

[7] *WHO guidelines for screening and treatment of precancerous lesions for cervical cancer prevention* (2013). Chapter 5: Screening and treatment of cervical pre-cancer. (Quote: "The procedure can be performed under local anaesthesia on an outpatient basis and usually takes less than 30 minutes.")

[8] Bilhimer, Matthew H. et al. (27. Feb. 2018): *Acute intoxication following Dimethyltryptamine ingestion.* In: Hindawi, Case Reports in Emergency Medicine, Article ID 3452691, Open Access. *https://www.hindawi.com/journals/criem/2018/3452691/ (accessed 23.01.2022)*

[9] Lucca, Adriano (2018): *Ayahuasca: A Near-death Transformation.* Discovery Publisher, New York

[10] Lamb, F. Bruce (1971): *Wizard of the Amazon: The Story of Manuel Córdova-Rios.*
North Atlantic Books, ISBN 978-0-938190-80-6, p.27

[11] Müller-Ebeling, Claudia, Arno Adelaars, Christian Rätsch (2006): *Ayahuasca: Rituale, Zaubertränke und visionäre Kunst aus Amazonien.* AT Verlag, ISBN 978-3038002703

[12] Romm, Aviva (2021): *Hormone Intelligence: The Complete Guide to Calming Hormone Chaos and Restoring your Body's Natural Blueprint for Well-Being.* HarperOne Publishers, ISBN 978-0062796219
[13] Hari, Johann (2018): *Lost Connections.* Bloomsbury Circus, ISBN HB: 978-1-4088-7868-2, p. 237
[14] Dr. Eric Berg (23.08.2020): *Practical Keto.* One of the many YouTube videos of Dr. Berg about the Ketogenic diet. *https://www.youtube.com/watch?v=tJICCFZLgHY (accessed 23.01.2022)*

Acknowledgements

I thank Ed Bear for bearing with me in my darkest hour and helping me to stay halfway sane. I would have lost my mind without him.

I thank Mr K. from the private clinic 1000 times for taking me in without an appointment and helping me to get to sleep after 155 hours of panic. His clinic is a safe haven and should be given Michelin stars.

Most of all, I thank my partner, Robyn Fox, for her all-round support, for listening to me, for helping me, for not abandoning me when I became grumpy and really strange for several months, for taking great photos of my ritual, for the first round of structural editing, for just about everything. I love you.

I also thank M. and E. for visiting me at the clinic and helping me with my first test run at 'normality'.

A special 'thank you' to my seven-month therapist, Ms. K. for helping me befriend all the additional, less severe monsters that rose to the surface which are not included in this book. After seven months, the effect of ayahuasca finally wore off.

I thank Martina Tyrrell for her excellent copy edit and her friendly and helpful tips aside from the 'job at hand'. I also thank Viktorija Martin, Claire Ellis, Lucy Reynolds and publishing director Helen Hart from the team at SilverWood Books for their great support, introducing me to the science of book publishing, answering so many questions and giving me so many tips, lists and useful recommendations. I can recommend them to any first-time book author. Michael Römer managed to turn my second-class iPhone snapshots into printable photos and turned my colour pencil drawings into printable illustrations. It was great to find a professional who understands colour the way I do.

I thank Karen Vogel, Vicky Noble and Lily Hillwomyn for their Motherpeace Round Tarot and Ffiona Morgan for her Daughters of the Moon Tarot. On 31st December 2017, two months before I even thought about going on an ayahuasca journey and six months before I went to Germany, I drew the Motherpeace card 'Six Sticks' and the Daughters of the Moon card 'Compassion/Six Cups' as my tarot cards for 2018. The first showed a wheel of fire with six fiery sticks pointing towards the centre. A naked shaman woman is standing in the centre with her hair standing on end, holding the symbol of a liana in her left hand and the symbol of a lion in her right hand (my adaptation is shown on the left). The second card showed a beach. On the left-hand side, a dark 'sea of emotions' filled five cups standing on the shoreline. On the right-hand side, a group of people had gathered around a woman who had fainted and dropped to the ground. A sixth empty cup stood beside her. The five compassionate people were attempting to revive her. I did not understand the cards at the time, and placed them face down in my bookshelf because I did not particularly like them, and promptly forgot about them until 31st December 2018 when I went looking for the two missing cards. What a surprise. They could not have been more accurate. Do I understand how reality works? No, I do not.

Left: My Adaptation of the "Six Sticks" Tarot Card

www.ingramcontent.com/pod-product-compliance
Lightning Source LLC
Chambersburg PA
CBHW040847170426
43201CB00005BB/46